Islam
on
Campus

A SURVEY OF UK STUDENT OPINIONS

Islam
on
Campus

A SURVEY OF UK STUDENT OPINIONS

by
John Thorne and Hannah Stuart

2008

THE CENTRE FOR SOCIAL COHESION

The Centre for Social Cohesion
Clutha House
10 Storey's Gate
London SW1P 3AY
Tel: +44 (0)20 7222 8909
Fax: +44 (0)5 601527476
Email: mail@socialcohesion.co.uk
www.socialcohesion.co.uk

The Centre for Social Cohesion
Limited by guarantee.
Registered in England and Wales: No. 6609071.

Printed in Great Britain by
The Cromwell Press
Trowbridge, Wiltshire

Contents

Introduction

Since 2006, the British government and the media have paid increasing attention to Muslim students at British universities following several high-profile cases where students or graduates took part in terrorist attacks or were convicted on terrorist-related charges. Several universities, prominent unions and Muslim groups have responded critically to these charges, accusing the government of initiating a witch-hunt against Muslims comparable with McCarthyism.[1]

There are some 90,000 Muslims presently studying at British universities. While several British Muslim students have indeed turned to terrorism, the issue is bigger than terrorism itself. The ideas, people and groups that individuals come into contact with during their university years inevitably help shape the rest of their lives. What Muslim students are thinking and doing now, and how they are perceived by their non-Muslim peers, will shape British society for at least a generation to come.

This report aims to improve public understanding of the issues surrounding Islam on campus and to discover the extent of Islamic radicalism at universities by asking students themselves. It is based on a YouGov poll of students opinions as well as on the ground research into a dozen university Islamic societies, exploring the views and experiences of Muslim and non-Muslim students on UK campuses during the academic year 2007/2008. The results show that Muslim students hold opinions and attitudes which are broad and varied, giving cause both for hope and concern.

---

1 For example, see 'Lecturers oppose Muslim 'witch-hunt', *The Daily Telegraph*, 02 June 2007. See: http://www.telegraph.co.uk/news/worldnews/1552951/Lecturers-oppose-Muslim-'witch-hunt'.html
'Universities urged to spy on Muslims', *The Guardian*, 16 October, 2006. See: http://www.guardian.co.uk/uk/2006/oct/16/highereducation.topstories3

Methodology

There are 2.3 million higher education students in Britain, an estimated 90,000 of them Muslim.[2] This report aims to present and analyse the views of British Muslim university students, and to describe their experience on campus. To do this, we followed several lines of research.

❖ **Online survey:** We conducted an online survey (carried out by the YouGov polling agency) of over 600 Muslim and over 800 non-Muslim students, posing questions on respondents' views of Islam and British society. Some questions were basic – i.e. "How often if at all do you attend Friday prayer?" – while others sought to elicit opinions about key issues such as religious tolerance, the role of women in society, the relationship between church and state, and current affairs.

❖ **Campus visits:** We also visited Freshers' Fairs, Muslim prayer rooms and Friday prayers, and attended Islamic Society talks at over a dozen universities around the UK. Where possible, prayers and talks were recorded and transcribed, and samples collected of literature distributed at events and in prayer rooms. Notes were taken of books available in prayer room book collections.

❖ **Interviews:** We conducted face-to-face interviews with current and recent Muslim university students. Interviewees included males and females, Islamic Society committee members and non-members, undergraduate and postgraduate students, converts to Islam, students of Pakistani, Arab, Bangladeshi, and Somali backgrounds, students who considered themselves conservative Muslims and students who said they barely practiced Islam at all.

Britain has over a hundred universities.[3] We chose to focus our research on a dozen high profile universities with significant Muslim student populations and active Islamic Societies.[4] While it is possible to draw generalisations, it is important to note that each university is unique, as is each Islamic Society.

This report covers the views and experiences on campus of Muslim university students in the UK. Therefore, it should not be considered a commentary on British Muslims generally.

---

2 'Student numbers and statistics', *Universities UK FAQs*. See: http://www.universitiesuk.ac.uk/faqs/showFaq.asp?ID=7#HowmanyHEstudentsarethereintheUK,
'The Voice of Muslim Students', *Federation of Student Islamic Societies*, August, 2005, p. 5. See: http://www.fosis.org.uk/resources/general%20literature/general%20literature/FullReport.pdf

3 'The higher education sector and UK universities', *Universities UK FAQs*. See: http://www.universitiesuk.ac.uk/faqs/showFaq.asp?ID=2

4 For a full list of universities visited please see appendix 4.

Background

■ Violent radicalism and British universities

Two of the most prominent radical Islamist groups active on British university campuses have been the UK-based al-Muhajiroun ("The Emigrants" - disbanded in 2004) and the UK branch of Hizb ut-Tahrir ("Liberation Party"), a worldwide organisation that promotes a political version of Islam and seeks to erect a global Islamic state.

Al-Muhajiroun was founded in 1996 by Lebanese-Syrian émigré Omar Bakri (Omar Bakri Mohammad Fostock) after he was expelled from Hizb ut-Tahrir.[5] In a December 2006 interview with *al-Sharq al-Awsat* newspaper, Bakri said he had delivered up to thirty talks a week on UK campuses between 1986 and 2004, concluding each with a call to embrace Islam and martyrdom.[6]

Following the September 11, 2001 attacks in New York and Washington D.C., al-Muhajiroun stalls appeared on campuses across Britain, where the group distributed leaflets promoting the idea of a grand clash between Islam and the West.[7] According to Bakri, al-Muhajiroun targeted over 48 universities and campuses – including Oxford, Cambridge, the London School of Economics (LSE) and King's College London (KCL). Anjem Choudary, another former leader of al-Muhajiroun, said in 2006 that "students of Omar Bakri still continue to preach in campuses."[8]

Bakri disbanded al-Muhajiroun in late 2004, and two successor groups, the Saved Sect and al-Ghurabaa, were banned by the British government following the July 7, 2005 suicide attacks in London under an amendment to the Terrorism Act in 2006.[9] Ahl us-Sunnah wal Jamma'ah, the most recent successor group to Al-Muhajiroun, was effectively broken up following the conviction in April 2008 of two

---

5 'Press statement regarding media coverage of *The Islamist*', *Hizb ut-Tahrir Britain*, 26 March, 2007, available at: http://www.hizb.org.uk/hizb/press-centre/press-release/press-statement-regarding-media-coverage-of-the-islamist.html

6 'The [Islamist] Groups and the Universities', *al-Sharq al-Awsat*, 15 December, 2006.
See: http://aawsat.com/details.asp?section=45&article=396859&issue=10244
See also 'Radical Islamist activities in UK campuses', *International Institute for Counter-terrorism*, 22 December, 2006. See: http://www.ict.org.il/apage/8286.php

7 'Muslim terror group linked to terrorist attacks', *The Guardian*, 19 September, 2001. See: http://education.guardian.co.uk/students/story/0,,554652,00.html

8 The [Islamist] Groups and the Universities', *al-Sharq al-Awsat*, 15 December, 2006.
See: http://aawsat.com/details.asp?section=45&article=396859&issue=10244
See also 'Radical Islamist activities in UK campuses', *International Institute for Counter-terrorism*, 22 December, 2006. See: http://www.ict.org.il/apage/8286.php

9 '"Muslims in Police will rise up", Bakri insists', *The Daily Telegraph*, 20 January, 2007. See: http://www.telegraph.co.uk/news/uknews/1540082/Muslims-in-police-will-rise-up%2C-Bakri-insists.html

of its key members – Abu Izzadeen (AKA Omar Brooks) and Simon Keeler – for fundraising for and inciting terrorism.

However, the UK branch of Hizb ut-Tahrir, founded in 1986 by Bakri and fellow Syrian Farid Kassim, is still active on British campuses. Following complaints by the National Union of Students (NUS) in the mid-1990s, some universities chose to ban the group from their campuses. In response, Hizb ut-Tahrir began operating through front organisations including the Muslim Media Forum, the Muslim Current Affairs Society, the 1924 Committee, the Comparative Ideology Society, and the New World Society. The group was banned entirely by the NUS in 2004 but has remained active on some campuses.[10]

Hizb ut-Tahrir and al-Muhajiroun have been linked to terrorist attacks carried out by Muslim students and former students of British universities since the mid-1990s. In some cases, those behind the attacks were also active in their universities' Islamic Societies:

❖ Amer Mirza, a British-born Humberside University accountancy student and alleged al-Muhajiroun member, was convicted in 1999 of petrol-bombing a British army base in Southall, London earlier that year to protest resumed U.S. bombing of Iraq.[11]

❖ Ahmed Omar Sheikh, a British-born former LSE student, was convicted in 2002 by a Pakistani court of the murder that year of Daniel Pearl, an American journalist for *The Wall Street Journal*. At LSE, Sheikh had reportedly been involved both with the university's Islamic Society and with Hizb ut-Tahrir – one of three al-Qaeda-linked terrorists who had studied at LSE, according to British security sources cited by *The Daily Telegraph*. "A number of students were brainwashed by outsiders," said an Islamic Society committee member quoted by *The Daily Telegraph*. "They did become very extreme."[12]

❖ British Muslims Asif Mohammed Hanif and Omar Khan Sharif carried out a suicide bombing that killed three and wounded 65 at a bar in Tel Aviv, Israel in April 2003.[13] According to Omar Bakri, Sharif had attended Bakri's talks for six months shortly before departing for Israel, although Bakri said Sharif was interested only in matters of theology, not combat.[14] Zaheer Khan, a friend of Sharif's, claims Sharif had first been radicalised by Hizb ut-Tahrir

10 'Islamic group in secret plan to recruit UK students', *The Independent*, 04 September, 2005. See: http://www.independent.co.uk/news/uk/crime/islamic-group-in-secret-plan-to-recruit-uk-students-505497.html 'Islamists "urge young Muslims to use violence"', *The Daily Telegraph*, 30 September, 2007. See: http://www.telegraph.co.uk/news/uknews/1564616/Islamists-'urge-young-Muslims-to-use-violence'.html

11 'Arab student is jailed for attack', *The Yorkshire Post*, 06 March, 1999.

12 'Al-Qaeda terror trio linked to London School of "Extremists"', *The Daily Telegraph*, 26 January, 2002. See: http://www.telegraph.co.uk/news/uknews/1382818/Al-Qa%27eda-terror-trio-linked-to-London-School-of-%27Extremists%27.html

13 'The British Suicide Bombers', *The Guardian*, 01 May, 2003, available at: http://www.guardian.co.uk/world/2003/may/01/israel5

14 'NS Profile – Omar Sharif', *The New Statesman*, 24 April, 2006, available at: http://www.newstatesman.com/200604240017

while studying maths at Kings College London.[15]

❖ Kafeel Ahmed died after driving a burning jeep packed with incendiary material into Glasgow airport in July 2007. Ahmed, originally from Bangalore, India, had studied aeronautical engineering at Queens University, Belfast where he served on the executive of the university Islamic society and was involved with the Islamic Student Society of Northern Ireland (ISSNI).[16] An Indian police commissioner suggested that Ahmed was radicalised between 2003 and 2005 whilst studying for a PhD in computational fluid dynamics at Anglia Ruskin University in Cambridge.[17]

In addition to those who have actually carried out attacks, several British Muslim university students have been convicted on terror-related charges ranging from incitement to actively plotting to commit violence. The following are a partial list of more prominent cases involving British Muslim students:

❖ Five British Muslims were jailed for life in April 2007 for conspiring to attack shopping centres and nightclubs in Britain using fertiliser-based explosives. One of the convicted, Jawad Akbar, was reportedly involved with a "militant Islamist political group" whilst studying mathematics, technology and design at Brunel University.[18] Brunel University refused to comment on the case of Akbar but denied that Islamic prayer meetings on campus were used for recruiting extremists. Anthony Garcia and Omar Khyam – also convicted – reportedly met at an Islamic fair at the University of East London in October 2002. During the trial the court heard that Garcia was radicalised after watching a video showing atrocities in Kashmir at the University of North London Islamic society meeting.[19]

❖ Waseem Mughal, a member of the University of Leicester Islamic society, was convicted with two other men in July 2007 of inciting murder through extremist websites. Mughal, a British-born biochemistry graduate who ran the Islamic society's website, was described by the court as engaging in "cyber jihad" by encouraging the murder of non-believers.[20]

❖ Yassin Nassari, then-president of the University of Westminster Harrow campus Islamic Society, was convicted in July 2007 of possessing articles useful to terrorists. Nassari had been arrested in May 2006 upon arrival from Amsterdam at London's Luton Airport. He was carrying bomb-making instructions and blueprints for the al-Qassam rocket used by Hamas militants in the Gaza strip against nearby Israeli towns. Police also found a computer hard-

---

15 'NS Profile – Omar Sharif', *The New Statesman*, 24 April, 2006, available at: http://www.newstatesman.com/200604240017

16 'Terror suspect told family "time had come"', *The Daily Telegraph*, 23 July, 2007.
See: http://www.telegraph.co.uk/news/uknews/1556736/Terror-suspect-told-family-'time-had-come'.html

17 'Questions arise about origins of terror plot in UK', *International Herald Tribune*, 08 July, 2007. See: http://www.iht.com/articles/2007/07/08/news/terror.php?page=1

18 'Profile: Jawad Akbar', *BBC*, 30 April, 2007. See: http://news.bbc.co.uk/1/hi/uk/6149788.stm

19 'Suspect: I prefer drink to koran', *The Daily Telegraph*, 26 September, 2006. See: http://www.telegraph.co.uk/news/uknews/1529835/Suspect-I-prefer-drink-to-Koran.html
'From bored youths to bombers', *The Times*, 02 May, 2007. See: http://www.timesonline.co.uk/tol/news/uk/crime/article1733893.ece

20 'Internet jihadists' jailed for 10 years', *The Guardian*, 05 July, 2007. See: http://www.guardian.co.uk/technology/2007/jul/05/terrorism.uknews

drive in his luggage containing documents about martyrdom and weapons training, as well as recordings of lectures by extremist clerics. During the trial, the court heard that Nassari had organized "radical" events for the Westminster Islamic Society.[21]

Furthermore, four Bradford University students and one schoolboy were jailed in July 2007 for possessing articles which could be used for terrorism after police found they had been downloading extremist material from the internet. The British students, whose convictions were overturned by the Appeal Court in February 2008, reportedly called on Muslims at a meeting of Bradford's Islamic Society in February 2006 to kill anyone who published the Danish cartoons of Muhammad. The Islamic Society subsequently expelled the students but did not report the incident to university authorities.[22]

In addition, in August 2006, Waheed Zaman, the British-born then-president of London Metropolitan University Islamic Society, was arrested in connection with an alleged plot to carry out suicide attacks against trans-Atlantic airliners.[23] Al-Muhajiroun literature and audio cassettes were found in the Islamic Society's offices.[24] At time of writing, the trial was still ongoing.

■ *Government response*

Government guidelines on combating Islamic extremism on university campuses were published in November 2006.[25] "There is evidence of serious, but not widespread Islamist extremist activity in HEIs (higher education institutions)," warned higher education minister Bill Rammell.[26] A leaked government document also

---

21 'Student's wife "encouraged him to become a terrorist"', *The Daily Telegraph*, 31 May, 2007. See: http://www.timesonline.co.uk/tol/news/uk/crime/article1862719.ece
See also 'The Trial of Yassin Nassari', Caged Prisoners website, 16 July, 2007. See: http://www.cageprisoners.com/articles.php?id=21104

22 'University launches review after conviction of student terror ring', *The Yorkshire Post*, 26 July, 2007. See: http://www.yorkshirepost.co.uk/news?articleid=3061619
'British students jailed for terrorism plans', *The Daily Telegraph*, 27 July, 2007. See:
http://www.telegraph.co.uk/news/uknews/1558664/British-students-jailed-for-terrorism-plans.html

23 'Airline plot suspects "inspired by 7/7 gang"', *The Times*, 09 April, 2008. See: http://www.telegraph.co.uk/news/uknews/1584216/Airline-plot-suspects-'inspired-by-77-gang'.html

24 'Inside this building, a terror suspect ran a London university's Islamic group. Was it also a recruiting ground for 'holy war'?', *The Sunday Telegraph*, 13 August, 2006. See: http://www.telegraph.co.uk/news/1526233/Inside-this-building%2C-a-terror-suspect-ran-a-London-university%27s-Islamic-group.-Was-it-also-a-recruiting-ground-for-%27holy-war%27.html

25 'Promoting Good Campus Relations: Working With Staff and Students to Build Community Cohesion and Tackle Violent Extremism In The Name of Islam at Universities and Colleges', Department for Education and Skills, November, 2006.
See: http://www.dfes.gov.uk/hegateway/uploads/ExtremismGuidancefinal.pdf

26 'UK defends student extremism guidelines', *Reuters*, 17 November, 2006. See: http://www.iol.co.za/index.php?set_id=1&click_id=24&art_id=qw1163764260678B226

claimed that Islamic societies had "a significant role in the extent of Islamic extremism on campus."[27]

The NUS praised the guidelines' "moderate tone" but warned that focusing solely on Islam could lead to a "racist or Islamophobic backlash."[28] The Federation of Student Islamic Societies (FOSIS) downplayed the alleged threat of Islamic extremism at universities. "If any terrorist activity took place, it would be reported. I just don't believe that any terrorist activity is taking place on campuses," said FOSIS spokesman Amar Latif.[29]

In May 2007, the University and College Union voted unanimously to reject government proposals that lecturers report students they suspected of "violent extremism in the name of Islam" to the police.[30]

In January 2008, the Department for Innovation, Universities and Skills issued updated guidance for preventing violent extremism on UK campuses. According to new government proposals, universities with large numbers of Muslim students should discourage religious segregation on campus and share information about violent Islamist speakers with a view towards barring them from addressing students.[31]

27 'Counter-terrorism unit to tackle campus extremism', *The Telegraph*, 24 October, 2006. See: http://www.telegraph.co.uk/news/uknews/1532087/Counter-terrorism-unit-to-tackle-campus-extremism.html

28 NUS press release regarding government guidelines, 17 November, 2006. See: http://resource.nusonline.co.uk/media/resource/VicLangerDfES.pdf

29 'UK defends student extremism guidelines', *Reuters*, 17 November, 2006. See: http://www.iol.co.za/index.php?set_id=1&click_id=24&art_id=qw1163764260678B226

30 'Lecturers refuse to spy on Muslim students', *The Guardian*, 30 May 2007, available at: http://education.guardian.co.uk/further/story/0,,2091374,00.html
'Tougher vetting of students needed to combat campus extremism, expert warns', *The Guardian*, 17 November, 2006. See: http://education.guardian.co.uk/higher/news/story/0,,1950744,00.html
See: http://www.dfes.gov.uk/hegateway/uploads/ExtremismGuidancefinal.pdf

31 'Promoting good campus relations, fostering shared values and preventing violent extremism in Universities and Higher Education Colleges', *Department for Innovation, Universities and Skills*, January 2008. See: http://www.dius.gov.uk/publications/extremismhe.pdf

PART ONE

ISLAMIC SOCIETIES IN THE UK

Islamic societies in the UK

■ *What is an Islamic society?*

Campus Islamic societies (ISOCs) provide Muslim (and non-Muslim) university students with the chance to come together for religious, educational and social events. In addition, ISOCs often oversee campus Muslim prayer rooms, organise on-campus Friday prayers, and raise money for charities. They are usually incorporated within their university's student union and the National Union of Students (NUS).

ISOCs typically consist of an elected leadership committee that organises activities, and a body of registered members. An individual's participation in an ISOC may vary from attending most events and prayers, to merely being included on the ISOC's email mailing list.

ISOCs are often seen as providing a "Muslim" voice on campuses. Many members also feel that ISOCs provide a useful means of meeting other Muslim students socially. Muna Mohamed, recently head sister of the London School of Economics (LSE) ISOC, says:[32]

> "The reason I came to the Islamic society is because it is sort of looking for that comfort when you come from somewhere new and have no friends, so you're looking for somebody which is somewhat similar to you."

Islamic societies often work in conjunction with other university societies generally. For example, at the University of Manchester, the ISOC works closely with the Palestinian Society, often co-hosting events and sharing email subscription lists.

Similarly, ISOCs sometimes work with other student societies on individual projects such as interfaith dialogue events. Yusuf, a Contemporary Politics postgraduate at LSE, says:[33]

> "We actually do have interfaith events [with other religious societies]. And this is just to remind ourselves, remind other people, just to let people know that yes we have our belief, but that doesn't preclude us from interacting with societies of other people, rather we should just be good citizens, good people … and act in good ways, and speaking to anyone really."

Many Islamic societies encourage their members to get involved in local and national students' unions. ISOC representatives enjoy prominent representation in the NUS.

---

32 Muna Mohammed was interviewed on the 13 March, 2008

33 Yusuf was interviewed on the 13 March, 2008

■ *Prayer rooms and literature*

Many ISOCs are based in their university's prayer room – either a designated Muslim prayer room or a multi-faith room. Some ISOCs advertise the prayer room as their headquarters, but how official this affiliation is varies from campus to campus. Some campuses also have a female, "sisters-only" prayer room, although these tend to be smaller and less well-appointed than male prayer rooms.

In addition to serving as places for prayer, many Muslim prayer rooms contain book collections – usually consisting of copies of the Quran and other religious texts, and books about Islam by modern writers. While religious texts are often in the original Arabic, other books are more likely to be in English or English translation.

Book collections tend also to be mixed in terms of Islamic interpretation – from books by leading Islamist ideologues to works by liberal-minded Sufis and apolitical scholars. There may also be disparity between collections set aside for male and female ISOC members in their respective prayer rooms.

For example, here are several titles observed among a collection of about 30 books in English in the male prayer room at the University of Birmingham in September 2007:

❖ Ibn Taymiyyah, *Essay on Servitude*, (Al Hidaayah Publishers & Distributors (UK) Publishing)
~ *The writings of medieval scholar Ibn Taymiyyah often cited by some modern Islamists and jihadists as a basis for their views.*

❖ Sayyid Abul A'la Mawdudi, Understanding Islam (Published in the U.S. as Towards Understanding Islam), (Kazi Publications)
~ *Sayyid Abul A'la Mawdudi was a seminal 20th-century Islamist thinker and founder of Pakistan's Jamaat-e-Islami party.*

❖ Abdul-Azeez Bin Baz (Sheikh), *The Correct Belief and its Opposite and What Negates al-Islam*, (al-Firdous Ltd., London) (2 copies)
~ *Abdul-Azeez Bin Baz served as Grand Mufti of Saudi Arabia from 1993 until his death in 1999.*

❖ Zainab Al-Ghazali, *Return of the Pharoah: Memoir in Nasir's Prison*, (Islamic Foundation, 2006, UK)
~ *Zainab Al-Ghazali, a prominent Egyptian Islamist writer associated with the Muslim Brotherhood, likens the secular pan-Arabist Nasser regime to one of Islamic tradition's great villains, the Pharaoh who held the Jews in bondage.*

❖ I.A. Ibrahim, *A Brief Illustrated Guide to Understanding Islam*, (2 copies) (Dar-us-Salam Publications; 2nd edition, May 1999.
~ *I.A. Ibrahim's guide to Islam has been published by Dar-us-Salaam Publications, a leading Saudi Arabian publishing house promoting Wahhabism.*

In comparison, a greater variety of Islamic viewpoints is on display among the forty-odd English-language titles in the same university's female prayer room, visited in January 2008:

Audio Cassettes:

❖ *Karbala: The Martydom of Hussain,* (Cherry Orchard Publications, UK)
 ~ *This cassette references the "martyrdom" in 680 A.D. of Mohammed's grandson Hussain in the initial Sunni-Shia conflict – a date still commemorated with mourning by minority Shias.*

❖ Hamza Yusuf, *Life and Character of the Prophet*

❖ Hamza Yusuf, *Dajjal & the New World Order*
 ~ *These two tapes are talks by Sheikh Hamza Yusuf Hanson, a prominent American Sufi scholar known increasingly for promoting religious tolerance and support for democracy.*

Books:

❖ Faraz Fareed Rabbani, *The Absolute Essentials of Islam* (White Thread Press, US)
 ~ *Canadian Sufi scholar Faraz Rabbani is a columnist with Islamica magazine.*

❖ Mawdudi, *Towards Understanding Islam* (Kazi Publications, March 1992, US) (6 copies)

❖ Mawdudi, *Witness into Mankind: The Purpose and Duty of the Muslim Ummah* (The Islamic Foundation, UK) (3 copies)
 ~ *Mawdudi, as noted above, was one of the last century's most influential Islamist thinkers.*

The disparity both between the brothers' and sisters' collections, and within the latter, suggest both that no one person regulates the book collections in the University of Birmingham's prayer rooms and that there may be little co-ordination between the men's and women's prayer rooms. We found similar situations at many other universities visited.

The lack of regulation of prayer room book collections can lead to disputes between students of different religious viewpoints. Ali al-Mawlawi, an International Studies and Diplomacy postgraduate at London's School of Oriental and African Studies (SOAS), describes one such disagreement between a Salafi student and a Sufi student at the University of Birmingham,[34] where al-Mawlawi was an undergraduate:[35]

"In the prayer room at our university there was almost a struggle as to what kind of books you were allowed in the prayer room. I remember there was, although they didn't know each other, there was a Salafi and a sort of traditional Sunni Sufi. And the Sunni Sufi would take the books that the other guy put in the prayer room, take them home basically. And then the Salafi would come and day 'could you please refrain from taking these books, we only have one each'. And there was that sort of underlying disapproval about what kind of books you could have in the prayer room ... I know definitely the, let's say, the Wahhabis would actively get books from ... publishers and to be honest I have found books which I consider to be offensive. But I can honestly say I haven't taken them out ... The problem I think is that there doesn't seem to be any strict regulations about who's allowed to put books in the prayer room."

---

34 Some militant Salafis regard the Sufist approach as heretical

35 Ali al-Mawlawi was interviewed on the 14 January, 2008

In addition, short tracts and leaflets about Islam and Islamic political issues are often on display in prayer rooms – usually left out in multiple copies to be taken away.

The management of prayer rooms by ISOC committees varies from university to university. Some ISOCs regulate the acquisition and display of reading material. Others do no more than oversee what current and previous members have donated. A few pay no attention at all to literature available in the prayer room. Faisal Hanjra, head of the Queen Mary (University of London) ISOC and media spokesman of the Federation of Student Islamic Societies (FOSIS), says:[36]

> "Often people just give in books, and it's up to the Islamic societies to make sure that they're screening these books and whatever that means."

■ *Friday prayer*

One of the main functions of an ISOC is organising the group prayer and *khutba*, or sermon, each Friday. Though the format for organising Friday prayers varies from campus to campus, prayers tend to be led either by an ISOC committee member or a guest speaker invited by the ISOC. Muna Mohamed, recently head Sister of the LSE ISOC, says:

> "We have a couple of people that generally give the *khutba* and then again recommendations from the brothers. For example, the ISOC presidents generally tend to give the **khutba** and then you get outside speakers."

The content of sermons varies widely. Some sermons deal with basic issues of practicing Islam. In one sermon delivered on the 25th January, 2008 at the University of Birmingham, the speaker stressed the importance of prayer:

> "How can we know we are going to be Muslims when we die? What keeps us being Muslims? What keeps us being Muslims is the prayer ... the point of the prayer is to get us closer to Allah, is to get closer to him inshallah."

Other sermons talk about the state of Islam either in the UK or in the world, and address how Muslims should take action to strengthen their faith. In one sermon delivered on the 8th February, 2008 at King's College London, the speaker warned listeners of a sense of weakening faith, urging them to get involved with their university's ISOC:

> "The Dejal [antichrist] will not appear until people forget about him and the Imam stops speaking about him ... This is why I am here today, to talk to you about a topic which is not talked quite very often in our [mosque] ... Our faith is weak ... Do not feel shy, there's brothers and sisters here that are ready to help you, there's brothers and sisters here that

---

36 Faisal Hanjra was the media spokesperson for FOSIS when interviewed on the 9 April, 2008. Hanjra was elected president of FOSIS in June 2008 at the FOSIS annual conference in Salford, Manchester. See 'Muslim Students Convene in Salford and Elect New Leaders', FOSIS press release, 30 June, 2008. See: http://www. fosis.org.uk/media/archives_read.php?id=145

you can readily approach and say I want to help, I want to be part of the ISOC, I want to do something for Islam, I want to do dawah, I wanna take part, I wanna please my lord."

Some sermons address political issues that that affect Muslims either in the UK or abroad. In a sermon delivered on the 11th January, 2008 at the University of Birmingham, the speaker compared the early Muslim community led by Mohammed to the "severed" Muslim community today, calling for worldwide Muslim solidarity:

"[Mohammed] established a new society, a new Muslim community on three very important issues. But that's the spirit of love and brotherhood, sacrifice on behalf of the Sahaba [prophet's companions] … Those people who were in Medina, they love those people who came in from Mecca. And they even prefer them to themselves, and they prefer them even to their children, and even they prefer them to their wife … [Now] sisters are delivering their babies at the Jewish checkpoints. What are we doing? Look at what's happening in Iraq. People are dying by their scores. It's a very simple situation. The body of the Muslim ummah has been severed and cut to pieces."

Many students prefer attending prayer at university rather than at a local mosque because the sermons at university are often more relevant to student lives. Faheem Javaid, a 3rd-year Maths student at Queen Mary, who prefers to attend Friday prayer on campus, says:[37]

"They talk about issues that are quite relevant to students … Anything nowadays, such as street life, exams etc. Issues that I relate a lot more to, rather than a lot of local mosques will talk about a lot of politics, and I think that is always a central issue, whereas I don't think it's always the most important."

However, Friday prayers can become points of contention, particularly when sermons promote intolerant attitudes. Some students express concern that sermons may fail to accommodate minority groups within Islam. Ali al-Mawlawi, a Shia International Studies and Diplomacy postgraduate at SOAS, says of sermons given at the university's prayer room:

"On a number of occasions they mentioned something about Shias … Even at SOAS the person giving out the sermon often says things that I personally wouldn't agree with, but I don't necessarily find it offensive, and I think that's the key. I mean I've always got used to the fact that there's going to be people standing up saying things that I don't personally agree with. For me, that's fine as long as they don't cross the boundary of respect and appreciate that there are other people at the Friday prayers that aren't traditional Sunnis and aren't traditional Salafis."

In addition to overseeing Friday prayers, many ISOCs also organise weekly discussion groups on Islam, and hold daily *Iftars* – the evening meal breaking the daily fast – or "iftar parties" during the Islamic holy month of *Ramadan*.

---

37 Faheem Javaid was interviewed on the 16 January, 2008.

■ *Social Events and Lectures*

Many ISOCs organise a variety of social events including "dawah events" (from the Arabic *da'wah*, or "inviting") to invite non-Muslims on campus to convert to Islam. Organising religious and educational lectures, however, is the primary activity of most ISOC. Like *khutbas*, lectures deal with issues ranging from points of theology and Islamic law, to practical advice for living as a Muslim, to current political issues affecting Muslims.

For example, in a November 2007 ISOC talk at SOAS, Canadian scholar Faraz Rabbani said that only qualified scholars should interpret Islamic law. In response to a question from the audience on how Muslims of different sects and opinions could resolve their differences, Rabbani said:

> "The challenge is not to resolve our differences; the challenge is to live with our differences … The problem is individual, angry voices that speak without qualification."

Other talks deal with the practicalities of being a Muslim in the United Kingdom, such as how to deal with perceived increased surveillance of Muslims by the police. At an ISOC talk titled "Know Your Rights" delivered on the 25th January, 2008 at University College London (UCL), the speaker argued that Muslims should retaliate by refusing to cooperate with police on tackling neighbourhood crime:

> "The police always say 'Well, we are doing what's best for the country'. This is why the police lobby, the security services lobby, have to be watched very carefully … We'll put the word out around the whole streets, everywhere in the country, that Muslims should not co-operate with the police. And what that in fact means is, most of the police's job isn't terrorism, it's ordinary crime. And they know as well that ordinary crime, for which they need the cooperation of the communities, not just Muslim, but Afro-Caribbean, white communities, any of the communities. We say, we'll put the word out and campaign that police have become anti-Muslim, they are political, no one will co-operate with you, all your statistics will go down the drain, you want to get drug dealers, you want to get burglars, then we'll see what we can do."

Some talks deal with how Muslims should relate to non-Muslims. While many speakers urge tolerance, some promote a hostile attitude towards those seen as non-Islamic. In an ISOC talk titled "The Return of Jesus" delivered on the 12th December, 2007 at Queen Mary, speaker Abu Mujahid argued that Muslims must love and hate according to God's will, singling out homosexuals for condemnation:

> "Love for the sake of Allah like you will hate for the sake of Allah, not the people who love everything and love everyone, that's not Islam, that is not Islam, but we love the one Allah loves and we love the place Allah loves and we love the things Allah loves, and we're at war and we hate the place Allah hates and the person Allah hates and the things that Allah hates, so we don't accept homosexuality … we hate it because Allah hates it."

In the same talk, Abu Mujahid argued that the present state of Christianity is a warning to Muslims not to adulterate their faith with what Abu Mujahid called "alien" influences:

"We excommunicate people … when they transgress their limits of God and ascribe partners to him or disbelieve in him … now what I demonstrated for you was appeasement and assimilation … Christmas for example, now clearly they arose around the 4th century where people accepted [non-Christian influences] to make these pagans more Christian … Look at the dangers of compromise, look at the dangers of appeasement, when you accept something from an alien or foreign tradition that is not from the core religion, down the line, decades, centuries, millennium after that, you're going to get a very rotten apple, and that's what I think the Christian world is suffering from."

Some talks deal with specific political issues affecting Muslims, notably the War on Terror, the Iraq and Afghanistan wars, and the Israeli-Palestinain conflict. In a speech delivered on the 29th November, 2007 at Queen Mary University, speaker Azzam Tamimi characterised the Palestinian struggle as a Muslim struggle:

"Let me tell you this, no suffering can deter the Palestinians from continuing their resistance to occupation. No pain, no collective or individual punishment will convince the Palestinians to give up their rights to their land and the whole land is Palestinian … Every single drop of sand is Arab and Muslim. Those who kicked my mother out of her house, and those who deny me the right to go back to my father's land, came from the foreign … from South Africa, from Britain, from France, from North America, from everywhere else but Palestine because they were in no use to Palestine before. It was the Zionists, atheists, secular, God denying communities of Eastern Europe, the pioneers of this project. The most inhumane project in the modern history of humanity … religion for us in the land of Islam and wherever there are Muslims is something else. Religion for us is part of our lives, we live by it and we live for it and we die for it."

After the speech, donations were collected for Interpal, a UK-based Palestinian charity currently under investigation by the Charity Commission for alleged links to Hamas, the militant Palestinian branch of the Muslim Brotherhood proscribed in the UK under the Terrorism Act 2000.[38] Interpal was banned in Israel in July 2008 due to alleged financial links to Hamas.[39]

■ *Charity Work*

As part of giving *zakat* – one of the five pillars of Islam, literally a wealth tax but more commonly understood as giving to charity – many ISOCs undertake a range of charitable activities including the provision of social and educational projects, as well as fundraising for Islamic charities. "Charity Week," a yearly fund-raising drive, is considered one of the most important activities of many ISOCs.

Our study found that the charitable work of ISOCs is seen as one of its most impor-

---

38 'Statement from the Charity Commission on the Palestinian Relief and Development Fund', *Charity Commission,* available at: http://www.charity-commission.gov.uk/news/intsate.asp
'List of proscribed terrorist groups under the Terrorism Act 2000', Home Office website. See: http://www.homeoffice.gov.uk/security/terrorism-and-the-law/terrorism-act/proscribed-groups

39 'Israel bans British group over "links to Hamas"', *The Times,* 09 July, 2008. See: http://www.timesonline.co.uk/tol/news/world/middle_east/

tant functions by ISOC members, many of whom expressed a desire to do something meaningful. Muna, recently head Sister at LSE ISOC, explains how the work done by previous ISOC members inspired her to get involved in her university's ISOC:

"One of those sisters was very very active and she even got an award at the end of her third year recognising throughout the year not just her contributions within the Islamic society but contributions to societies in general. And a lot of what she did, she did for religious reasons and I found that passion and willingness to help and go out of her way to do something … that was very inspiring for me."

■ *The Federation of Student Islamic Societies (FOSIS)*

The Federation of Student Islamic Societies in the UK and Ireland (FOSIS), founded in 1962, is an umbrella grouping of most major university Islamic societies in the UK that aims to support and represent Muslim students in higher and further education in the UK.[40]

According to its prospectus, available at Freshers' Fairs, FOSIS' stated aim is "to unify and mobilise Islamic Societies, as well as empower and represent Muslim students." Elsewhere, FOSIS claims to "bring these students together, to share experiences and to offer help and advice where appropriate, uniting Muslim students to positively contribute to both Muslim and non-Muslim communities alike."[41]

There are indications that FOSIS grew out of Islamist activism in 1960s Britain. In a 1964 letter to researcher Marika Sherwood, Hoossain Rajah, then a student at Manchester University, described leading Muslim Brotherhood member Said Ramadan as "the brain behind the formation of...FOSIS."[42] Writer and critic Ziauddin Sardar, who served as FOSIS Secretary General in the early 1970s, says:[43]

"Most members of FOSIS ... [were] ... strongly influenced by the Muslim Brotherhood of Egypt and Jamaat-e-Islami of Pakistan. These organisations preached a simple message: Islam Good; Secularism Bad."

FOSIS is made up of members and former members of individual ISOCs. President of Queen Mary ISOC and FOSIS media spokesman, Faisal Hanjra, says:

"It's very much a membership body. Islamic societies prescribe to the organisation. And every year they get to vote in a new executive and so on and so forth. So the new executive every year is pretty much made up of former Islamic society presidents, or individuals who have been involved in the Islamic society in the past."

---

40 'Introduction', *FOSIS* website. See: http://www.fosis.org.uk/about/intro_to_fosis.php

41 'The Voice of Muslim Students: A report into the attitudes and perceptions of Muslim students following the July 7th London attacks', FOSIS. August 2005.

42 'Malcolm X in Manchester and Sheffield', *North West Labour History Journal*, Vol. 27, 2002, p. 31

43 'Searching for Secular Islam', *New Humanist*, Vol. 19, Issue 5, Sept/Oct 2004. Please see: http://newhumanist.org.uk/798

FOSIS works with Islamic societies in a variety of ways, as Hanjra explains:

> "[FOSIS] has a very good working relationship with Islamic societies across the country, naturally because Muslim students are so spread out, it's not always possible to speak to every single Islamic society on the ground, but it has a very good working relationship with a lot of them, and it provides a variety of different things, it provides solicitors, advice, it provides more Islamic society based things such as speakers, materials, freshers' fair, all kind of different things."

FOSIS' services committee provides strategic and structural advice, co-ordinating the Muslim delegation for NUS conferences and organising an annual conference featuring workshops, sports activities and lectures. FOSIS also uses its national status to help ISOCs arrange for Muslim speakers of international renown they might otherwise not have been able to secure. Hanjra says:

> "Sometimes we have very good links with international speakers across the world, as a major organisation we have the ability to bring those speakers out"

FOSIS actively encourages Muslim students to join their university ISOC and to get involved in student politics. However, Hanjra believes that too many Muslim students are not sufficiently engaged in political issues:

> "They're [Muslim students] politically very apathetic, except for the occasional international issue like Palestine or Iraq, but just generally very apathetic … It is crucially important that Muslim students get on the page right now, get on the ball right now, because these debates are being had around us right now, policies are being passed around us right now, and if Muslim students don't take part in that debate, before we know it we are going to wake up tomorrow … all this legislation will be in place and we wouldn't have impacted on it at all."

Hanjra further believes ISOCs and FOSIS ought to encourage more political involvement on campus, saying:

> "I think the Islamic societies and organisations like FOSIS play quite a role in that about educating Muslim students that we can get a lot of support around issues of pre-trial detention, on issues of Iraq war, issues of Palestine, so very emotive issues."

FOSIS also supports – and often coordinates – ISOCs' fundraising for charity. Charities endorsed by FOSIS include Muslim charities such as Muslim Hands, Muslim Aid, Islamic Relief and Islamic Aid, as well as non-Islamic charities including Human Appeal International, Helping Hands Worldwide, Human Relief Foundation and Cancer Research UK.[44]

In addition, FOSIS promotes fund-raising by ISOCs for the charity Interpal, whose stated aim is to raise funds for projects delivering humanitarian aid to both Palestinians within territories under the control of the Palestinian Authority, and Palestinian refugees in Lebanon, Jordan and Syria.[45]

---

44 FOSIS website: links section. See: http://www.fosis.org.uk/links.php

45 'Our Projects', *Interpal*, available at: http://www.interpal.org/ourprojects/ourprojects.html

FOSIS and links to other national Islamic organisations

FOSIS has strong links with a variety of national Islamic organisations including the Muslim Council of Britain (MCB), the Muslim Association of Britain (MAB), Jamiat Ihyaa Minhaaj Al-Sunnah (JIMAS), the educational foundation Utrujj and the Islamic Foundation (IF). Hanjra says:

> "We have a good working relationship with all the major Muslim organisations in the UK, in a variety of deals, be it encouraging people to get democratically involved, be it to invite issues etc."

The group's website suggests that such links to national Islamic organisations make FOSIS "one of the largest, if not the largest representative organisation of Muslim youth in the UK", which, by extension, "represents the views of Muslim students to the media."[46]

Islamic societies nationwide are at least nominally affiliated, via FOSIS, to the Muslim Council of Britain (MCB), a registered charity and umbrella group which claims over 400 affiliates and describes itself as the largest Muslim organisation in the UK. Since its 1997 founding, the MCB has sought to position itself as the main voice of British Muslims. Yet, according to a 2006 Dispatches poll, 'What Muslims want', for Channel 4, less than 4% think that the MCB represents British Muslims.[47] In addition, many of the group's leaders and founders such as Khurshid Ahmad were formerly affiliated with Islamist parties in Pakistan such as Jamaat-e-Islami.[48]

FOSIS – and by extension ISOCs – also enjoy strong ties with the Muslim Association of Britain (MAB), widely considered a British branch of the Muslim Brotherhood. A 2005 FOSIS publication claims these links help to foster greater tolerance within such organisations:[49]

> "The involvement of many former FOSIS activists has helped in establishing an inclusive and broad-based ethos within other organisations such as the Muslim Association of Britain and the Muslim Council of Britain."

However, FOSIS and its constituent Islamic societies regularly book MAB leaders and activists, many of whom publicly support the Muslim Brotherhood, to speak on university campuses. One such speaker, Azzam Tamimi, a Hamas supporter,[50]

---

46 'Introduction', *FOSIS* website. See: http://www.fosis.org.uk/about/intro_to_fosis.php

47 'Analysis of the Muslim survey', *Dispatches, Channel 4*, 07 August, 2006. See: http://www.channel4.com/news/articles/dispatches/kenan+malik+analysis+of+the+muslim+survey/158240

48 'Radical Links of UK's 'Moderate' Muslim Group', *The Observer*, 14 August, 2005. See: http://www.guardian.co.uk/uk/2005/aug/14/religion.immigrationpolicy

49 'The Voice of Muslim Students: A report into the attitudes and perceptions of Muslim students following the July 7th London attacks', FOSIS. August 2005.

50 Azzam Tamimi, a Palestinian, worked as spokesman for the Jordanian Muslim Brotherhood from 1989 to 1992, and has also been identified as a member of Hamas, the Brotherhood's Palestinian branch. (Please see: *Commons Hansard*, 18 December 2003, Column 1763, remarks by Louise Ellman MP)

said in a BBC interview in 2006, "if I can go to Palestine and sacrifice myself I would do it."[51]

Other national Islamist organisations offer ISOCs practical support, training and advice. For example, the College Link Project (CLP) was created in 1994 by the Young Muslim Organisation UK (YMO UK) and Muslimaat UK, the youth wing of the Islamic Forum Europe (IFE), to support student Islamic societies on British university campuses. The project provides training in *da'wah* and preaching, and organises annual Muslim Student Awards (MSA). Launched in 2002, the awards programme aims to counter perceived Islamophobia on campuses, and is also supported by the MCB, the IF and the London Borough of Tower Hamlets.[52]

FOSIS and Friends of Al-Aqsa

FOSIS provides ISOCs with literature – Freshers and Dawah packs, leaflets on Islamophobia and pamphlets on political issues such as Palestine, Kashmir and Iraq – many of which are published by Friends of Al-Aqsa, a lobby group campaigning against alleged human rights abuses by Israel that advocates the creation of a single Palestinian state to replace Israel and the Palestinian Territories. Leaflets produced by Friends of Al-Aqsa include "Israeli War Crimes" and "Israeli Apartheid Policies", and much of the literature calls for a boycott of Israeli products and academic institutions.[53]

Founded in 1997, Friends of Al-Aqsa's stated goals include "defending the human rights of Palestinians and protecting the sacred al-Aqsa Sanctuary in Jerusalem."[54] Ismail Patel, the current leader of Friends of Al-Aqsa, has said that the group aims "to raise awareness of the Palestinians' sufferings and dispel the notion that Hamas is barbaric, and that it cannot be dealt with."[55]

Patel is a regular spokesman for the British Muslim Initiative (BMI),[56] founded in 2006 by prominent members of the MAB – the Muslim Brotherhood's British franchise.[57] Patel also sits on the advisory board of the Conflicts Forum,[58] a pressure group that promotes the Muslim Brotherhood to policy-makers in the West, and is

---

51 'Anger over radical's suicide bomb boast', *The Daily Mail*, 21 August, 2006. See: http://www.dailymail.co.uk/news/article-401635/Anger-radicals-suicide-bomb-boast.html

52 Muslim Students Awards Information pack. See http://www.muslimstudentawards.com/live/pdf/5,1,0.pdf

53 For a full list of Friends of Al-Aqsa leaflets found on UK campuses during the academic year 2007/08 see appendix 3.

54 'About Us', *Friends of Al-Aqsa* website. See: http://www.aqsa.org.uk/FRIENDSOFALAQSA/AboutUs/tabid/91/language/en-US/Default.aspx

55 Ismail Patel, speaking at an Action Palestine event at the University of Manchester, 10 November, 2007. The Centre for Social Cohesion attended and recorded this event.

56 'Give us the freedom to disagree with you', *The Independent*, 04 July, 2007.

57 The Muslim Association of Britain was founded in 1997 by Kemal Helbawy, European spokesman for the Muslim Brotherhood. See: Abedin, Mahan, 'How to Deal with Britain's Muslim Extremists? An interview with Kamal Helbawy', *Global Terrorism Analysis*, Volume 3, Issue 7, 05 August, 2005

58 'Who we are', *Conflicts Forum* website. See: http://conflictsforum.org/who-we-are/ismail-patel/

a director of IslamExpo.[59]

Speaking at an event in November 2007 organised by the University of Manchester Palestinian society, Patel argued that a Palestinian state could only exist at the expense of the Jewish one.

Patel said he considered the creation of Israel within its original borders as much a military invasion as the occupation of the West Bank and the Gaza strip after the Six-Day War. Patel argued that both stages of occupation had to be undone for any sort of Palestinian state to exist – in other word, a two-state solution is not possible. He said:

> "[It is my] personal belief that if a crime committed in 1967 cannot be forgiven, then a crime committed in 1948 cannot be forgiven."

At the same event, Patel pledged his support for Hamas, the militant Palestinian wing of the Muslim Brotherhood designated a terrorist organisation by the United States, the UK and the European Union. Answering an audience question about his views on Hamas, Patel said:

> "I think [Hamas] is one of the noblest resistance movements I've come across."

Patel added that Hamas had taken "the path of democracy in January 2006." Referring to Hamas' victory in Palestinian parliamentary elections, he said:

> "[Since January 2006] none of the activities of Hamas or its military wing went outside the Palestinian territories. They have only attacked the occupiers – nobody else."

At the same event Patel said:

> "Student societies are extremely important because of what [students] will become. They will shape the thinking of people in power."

---

59 'IslamExpo Launch', *IslamExpo* website. See: http://islamexpo.info/index.php?option=com_content&task=view&id=59&Itemid=1

PART TWO

SURVEY OF UK STUDENT ATTITUDES AND OPINIONS

Islam on campus

■ Membership of Islamic societies

A quarter (25%) of Muslim students polled said they were members of their university's ISOC. By contrast, only 6% of non-Muslim students polled said they belonged to a religious society. ISOCs tend to be peopled largely by young, Sunni undergraduates.

Diagram 1: Are you a member of your university's Islamic Society?

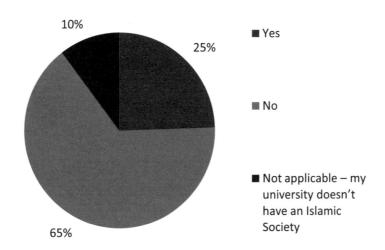

- ■ Yes
- ■ No
- ■ Not applicable – my university doesn't have an Islamic Society

Undergraduate students (29%) are almost twice as likely as postgraduates (16%) to belong to their ISOC. Correspondingly, respondents aged 18 – 34 (hereafter "younger") (26%) were over twice as likely as respondents aged 35 – 54 (hereafter, "older") (12%) to say they were ISOC members. Data from Sunnis and Shias, the two largest Muslim sects, registered roughly equal rates of ISOC membership (27% and 28% respectively) and men and women were almost equally likely (25% and 24% respectively) to say they were ISOC members.[60]

Muslim students were asked how active they were in their campus Islamic society. Just under half of ISOC members polled (45%) said they considered themselves active in the society: 8% are ISOC committee members; a tenth (10%) attend all the meetings and events; and over a quarter (27%) attend most of the meetings and events – hereafter referred to as "active" ISOC members. The remainder (54%) said they were not very active or not active at all and 1% were unsure.

---

60 Whilst the likelihood of Sunnis and Shias joining their university's ISOC is comparable, membership is overwhelmingly Sunni because a large majority – four fifths (79%) – of Muslim students are Sunni.

Diagram 2: And how active would you say you were in the Islamic Society?

I'm a committee member of my Islamic Society	8%
Very active – I go to all of the meetings and events	10%
Fairly active – I go to most of the meetings and events	27%
Not very active – I go to some meetings and events but not many	33%
Not at all active – I'm a member but I never attend meetings or events	21%
Not sure	1%

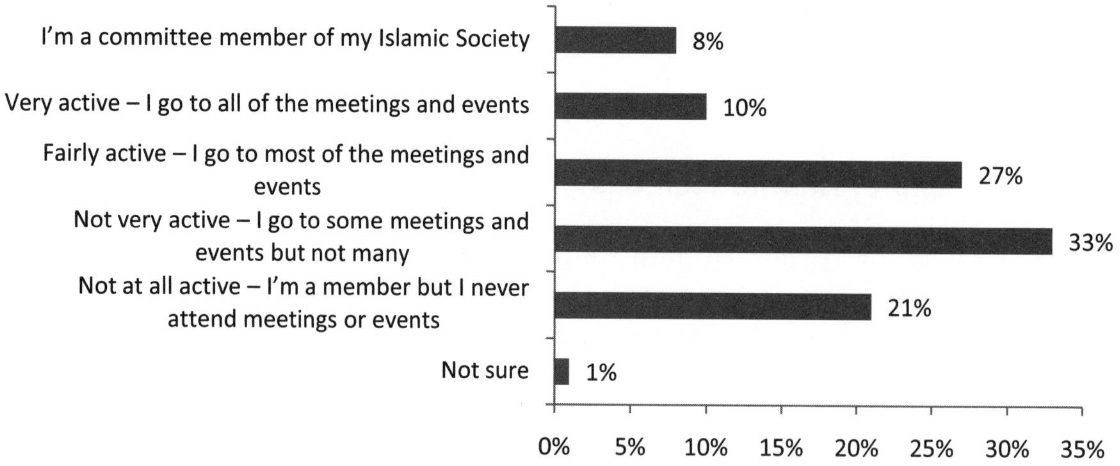

ISOC members tend to measure how active they are in their ISOC by how often they attend or help organise prayers and events. Usually, the more active a member is, the greater influence they have within the ISOC. Faheem Javaid, a 3rd year Maths student at Queen Mary (University of London), says:

> "There is a big difference in terms of who active participants are in the ISOC, in the sense that there are a lot more people who are active in organising the events, they take their time out in the day to set up the prayer room, set up the khutba, to get all the microphones and that ready, to get everything sorted out. Obviously in that sense, because obviously they are a lot more active ... they play a bigger role."

Diagram 3: And how active would you say were in the Islamic Society?

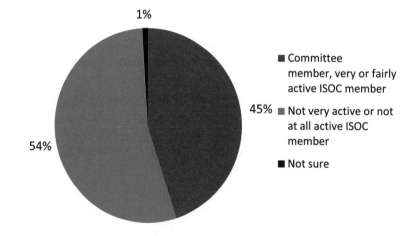

- ■ Committee member, very or fairly active ISOC member — 45%
- ■ Not very active or not at all active ISOC member — 54%
- ■ Not sure — 1%

ISOC leaders often place high priority on attracting new members. Muna Mohamed, recently head sister of the LSE ISOC, says:

> "The whole point of the ISOC is ... providing a service for some people that are active Muslims and practicing Muslims and then going out there to attract people who are on the fence."

Other students express a desire to broaden ISOCs' appeal to non-Muslims. Ali al-

Mawlawi, an International Studies and Diplomacy postgraduate at SOAS who is not actively involved in his university ISOC, says:

> "I'd actually like to see more events that are more inclusive I think, towards non-Muslims. A lot of the events I feel cater towards the Muslim communities in SOAS, but maybe not so relevant towards non-Muslims ... I feel that Muslims need to show that they're actually not just interested in Muslim issues, they are interested in issues which aren't exclusive to Muslims. But I think to be fair to them, the reason why they do it is because they feel it is their job to be dealing with Muslim issues, and maybe they don't have enough time to concentrate on other issues."

■ *The role of Islamic societies on campus*

Respondents were asked what roles ISOCs play on campus. The aim of this question was to gauge how ISOCs are viewed regarding their traditional functions of providing a voice for Muslim students, a Muslim social hub, a means for Muslim students to engage with other religious societies, and a venue for Muslim students to discuss and debate different ideas. Respondents were asked to say whether they felt a series of broad statements were true of the ISOC at their university.

Diagram 4: From what you know about your university's Islamic Society, which, if any, of the following statements do you generally agree with?

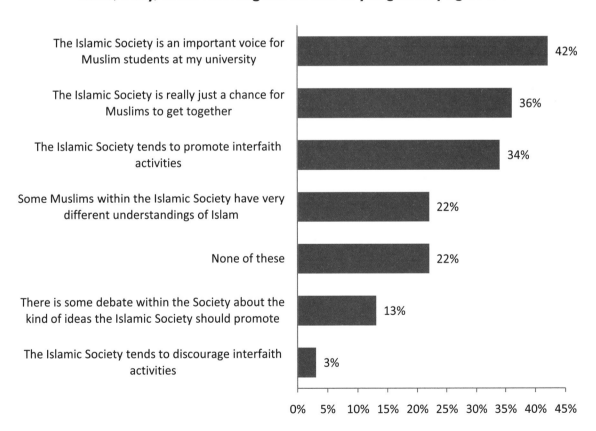

"The Islamic Society is an important voice for Muslim students at my university."

Over two fifths of Muslim students polled (42%) said the ISOC was "an important voice for Muslim students at my university." Interestingly, an even greater proportion of non-Muslim students polled (58%) held this view. But the group most supportive was active ISOC members (75%).

"The Islamic Society is really just a chance for Muslims to get together."

Over a third of Muslim students polled (36%) said the Islamic Society was "really just a chance for Muslims to get together." Muslim females (39%) were more likely than males (32%) to hold this view. Non-ISOC members (38%) were also more likely than active members (28%) to see their university's ISOC as a social institution rather than a purely religious one.

"The Islamic Society tends to promote interfaith activities"
(e.g. between Muslims, Jews, Hindus and Sikhs, etc.)

A third of Muslim students polled (34%) said that the ISOC at their university "tends to promote interfaith activities (e.g. between Muslims, Jews, Hindus and Sikhs, etc.)." Younger (age 18-34) Muslim students (37%) were more likely than older (age 35-54) Muslim students (16%) to agree, as were active ISOC members (63%) compared to non-members (28%). In general, those respondents more involved with the ISOC were more likely to say that their ISOCs promoted interfaith activities.

"Some Muslims within the society have very different understandings of Islam."

Over a fifth (22%) of Muslims polled agreed. Younger (age 18-34) students (23%) were more likely than older (age 35-54) students (10%) to agree. Active ISOC members (30%) were also more likely than non-members (21%) to agree.

Most young Muslim students interviewed described religious differences in terms of external signs of piety, particularly observing the five daily prayers or, for women, wearing the hijab. For others how religious you are is not something that can be outwardly measured. Jinan, a 3rd year Law student at the LSE, says:[61]

> "Only God knows how practicing you are, I can perhaps come in wearing full niqab and you will see me I am 24/7 in the prayer room like I'm praying all the time and you might see me as 'Oh my god, she is so practicing', but then God wouldn't see that as very practicing, maybe somebody who's just wearing hijab or whatever but if they are doing something for the community in God's eyes that person is someone who is more practicing."

Furthermore, many Muslim students see ISOCs as dominated by more conservative Muslims. Some believe ISOCs can repel potential members by being too strict. Junaid, a male 3rd-year Maths student at Queen Mary, says:[62]

---

61 Jinan was interviewed on the 13 March, 2008.

62 Junaid was interviewed on the 16 January 2008.

"[The ISOC] They're strict, they may be seen as strict, but the thing is they're very judge-mental as well … Because if I'm seen ever walking down with someone, if it's a girl, they won't even look at me."

Some Muslim students feel that ISOCs could gain members by being less conservative. Junaid says:

"[The ISOC] They will get a hell of a lot more, because I know for a fact that there's a good couple of thousand students here, and under 200 active members of ISOC … because their advertising had too much to do with 'look, you have to be a Muslim to pray 5 times a day'"

**"There is some debate within the society about the kind
of ideas the Islamic Society should promote."**

13% of Muslim respondents agreed. Overall, those respondents most involved with the ISOC – active ISOC members (32%) were the likeliest to agree.

**"The Islamic society tends to discourage interfaith activities"
(e.g. between Muslims and Jews, Hindus and Sikhs, etc.)**

3% of respondents agreed. Male Muslims (6%) were three times more likely than female Muslims (2%) to agree.

"None of these."

22% of respondents agree with none of the above statements. Overall, those least likely to agree were active ISOC members, while those most likely to agree were older (age 35-54) students and non-ISOC members. In other words, those respondents least involved with the ISOC tended not to have formed strong opinions about its role.

■ *Visiting campus prayer rooms*

Muslim students were asked how often, if at all, they visited the campus prayer room. Responses indicate considerable polarisation. Over a third (35%) of Muslim students use their campus prayer room regularly – 17% go at least once a day, 10% between two and five times a week and 8% once or twice a week. A further third (35%) have never visited their campus prayer room. The remainder visit less regularly – 6% use it once or twice a month and 8% less than once a month – or they attend a university that does not have a prayer room.

Active ISOC members polled tended to use their university's prayer room more often than non-ISOC members. Moreover, the data indicates that while active ISOC members visit their prayer room often, non-members use the facility seldom to never. At one end of the spectrum, 51% of active ISOC members said they used their campus prayer room daily, as compared with only 12% of non-ISOC members. At the other extreme, nearly half (49%) of non-ISOC members said they had never visited their campus prayer room, as compared to only 2% of active ISOC members.

For many active ISOC members, the campus prayer room is a hub of both religious and social life. However, even students interviewed who said they were not regular prayer room users felt it important that such a facility be available. Ali al-Mawlawi, an International Studies and Diplomacy postgraduate at SOAS says:

"[The prayer room] is very important. Because first of all it strengthens relationships between Muslims and the university, I think if there wasn't a prayer room then people would have to go outside the grounds to go, and that would be very inconvenient, but also I don't think the Muslims would get to know each other as well as if there wasn't a prayer room."

Diagram 5: How often, if at all, do you visit the campus prayer room at your university? A comparison of active ISOC members and non-members

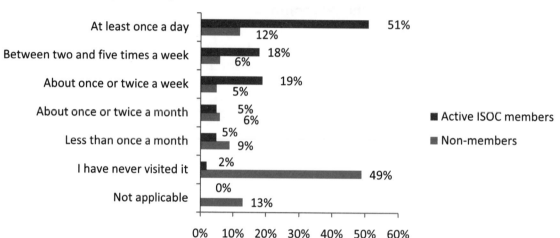

Attending Friday prayer

Muslim students were asked how often, if at all, they attended Friday prayer. Over two fifths of Muslim students polled (42%) said they regularly attend Friday prayer – 26% always attend and 16% nearly always attend. A minority of Muslim students polled (16%) attend Friday prayer occasionally and over two fifths (42%) attend rarely-to-never – 15% attend rarely and just over a quarter (27%) never attend Friday prayer. Females were overwhelmingly (44%) more likely than males (8%) never to go to Friday prayer, as were non-ISOC members (33%).

Overall, Friday prayer is most popular among active male ISOC members. Interviews and prayer room visits strongly supported this finding. As with general prayer room use, there was little middle ground; students polled either tended to attend Friday prayers often, or seldom-to-never. Female Muslim students were consistently less likely to attend Friday prayer and over five times more likely never to attend than male Muslim students.

Only a small proportion of regular attendees at Friday prayer are female. Zeynab el-Murad, a 3rd-year Maths student at Queen Mary who seldom attends Friday prayer, says:[63]

---

63 Zeynab el-Murad was interviewed on the 16 January, 2008.

"For girls it's much less important to attend Friday prayers. Well, it's not less important, but it's non-compulsory. Some believe it's compulsory of men,"

Diagram 6: And how often if at all do you attend Friday prayer? A comparison of male and female Muslim students

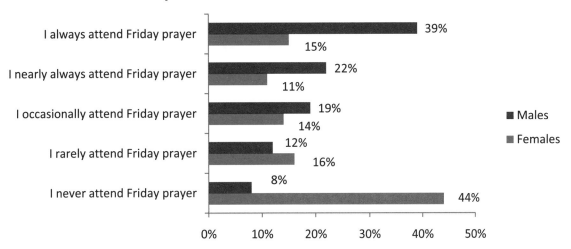

■ *Friends and social groups*

Respondents were asked to say which of a series of statements came closest to describing their social group. Over a third (37%) of Muslim students chose 'Some of my friends at university are Muslim, but I have friends from all sorts of different backgrounds'; a further third (38%) chose 'Religion is not an issue when I choose my friends at university.'

Almost one in ten (8%) Muslim students polled felt that the statement 'Most of my friends at university are Muslim, because I have more in common with them than I do with non-Muslims' most closely reflected their social group. Of the remainder, 4% chose 'Very few of my friends at university are Muslim; there aren't many Muslims at my university'; 5% chose 'Very few of my friends at university are Muslim; I find I have more in common with non-Muslims'; and 8% were unsure.

Three quarters of respondents (75%), therefore, felt that the following two statements best reflected their social group: 'Some of my friends at university are Muslim, but I have friends from all sorts of different backgrounds' and 'Religion is not an issue when I choose my friends at university'.

Diagram 7: Thinking about your university friends, which of the following statements comes closest to describing your social group?

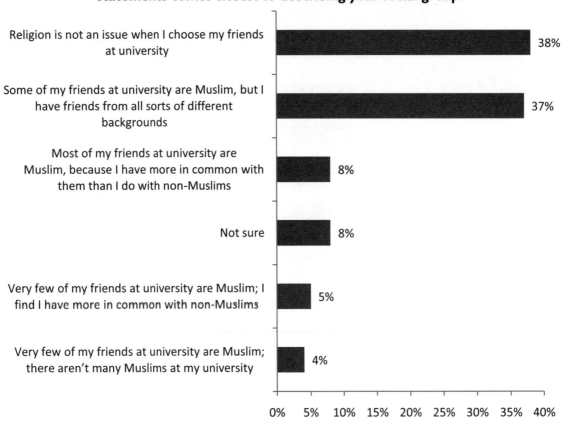

For some Muslim students, making friends can be dictated as much by the practical side of living an Islamic life as by deliberate choices on who to associate with. Yusuf, a Contemporary Politics postgraduate at the LSE, says:

"I think, at least for me for example, because if I pray, in many cases is with non Muslim friends said 'OK I have to go pray', and maybe they're like 'I want to go to the pub', or something like that … I'm not going to hang out with people who drink, and who don't pray. I mean even if I hung out with them, I myself would not drink and I would have to go pray, so a lot of times I don't impose, or judge people per se"

Amongst active ISOC members, however, over half (53%) said 'Some of my friends at university are Muslim, but I have friends from all sorts of different backgrounds' and 19% said 'Religion is not an issue when I choose my friends at university.' Active ISOC members (25%) were also five times more likely than non-members (5%) to say 'Most of my friends at university are Muslim, because I have more in common with them than I do with non-Muslims.' It appears that regardless of whether they consider it a factor in choosing friends, active ISOC members are more aware of their friends' religion.

Diagram 8: Thinking about your university friends, which of the following statements comes closest to describing your social group? A comparison of active ISOC members and non-members

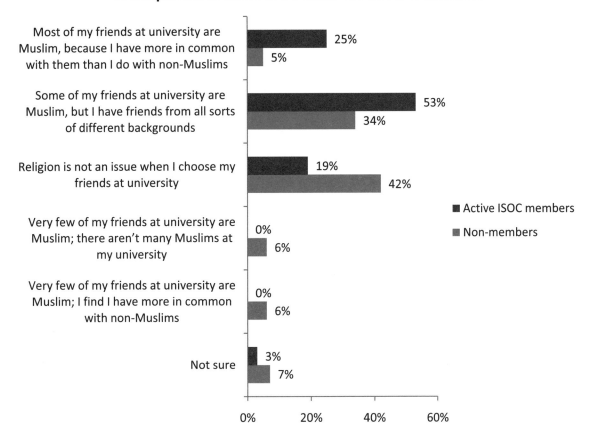

Views on Islam

■ Islam: religion or a way of life

Muslim students were asked whether they felt Islam was a religion, a way of life or both. A slim majority of respondents (52%) said Islam is both a religion and a way of life.

Diagram 9: Do you tend to think of Islam as a religion or a way of life?

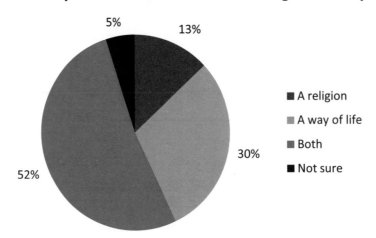

Active ISOC members (63%) were more likely to believe so compared to non-members (52%). Female Muslim students (55%) were more likely to agree than males (48%). Almost a third (30%) believe Islam is a way of life compared to almost one in eight (13%) Muslim students who believe Islam is primarily a religion. 5% of respondents were unsure.

For the majority of Muslim students in the UK, Islam is more than a religion. Muna Mohamed, recently head sister of the LSE ISOC, says:

> "For me Islam is more than a religion. I don't think it's as institutionalised … It has a say or influence in every aspect of your life. For instance talking to you could be religion for me. Going to the shops, do you know what I mean? So it's a way of life in that it dictates pretty much everything that I do."

■ Islam vs. Islamism

Islamism is a modern movement within Islam, often identified with such twentieth century ideologues as Sayyid Qutb and Abul A'la Mawdudi, and their respective organisations, the Muslim Brotherhood and Jamaat-i-Islami. Islamist doctrine states that Islam is necessarily political, and calls upon Muslims to make their religion a political project. Islamism typically envisions the creation of the Caliphate, a Muslim super-state governed according to strict Islamic law and values. This state would be in conflict with non-Muslim states. Islamist movements differ on how best to achieve this aim, some espousing militancy, others participation in democratic party politics, and others grass roots activism.

Respondents were asked to say which of two statements came closest to describing their view on Islam and politics. Over a sixth (15%) of respondents said that Islam and Islamism were part of the same thing and that politics is a big part of Islam. Twice as many active ISOC members (32%) held this view. By contrast, only 13% of non-ISOC members agreed. Over a third of overall respondents (36%) drew a clear line between Islam and Islamism. However, an even greater percentage of non-Muslim students polled (41%) did so.

Diagram 10: Islam and Politics: Which if any of the following statements comes closer to your view?

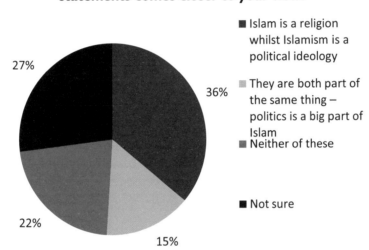

Just under a quarter of respondents (22%) said that Islam was neither a religion nor a political ideology. Postgraduate students (28%) were more likely to hold this view than undergraduates (20%). Over a quarter (27%) of respondents were unsure about the relationship between Islam the religion and Islamism the political ideology. Undergraduates (29%) were more likely than postgraduates (20%) to be so.

There is a variety of opinion about the relationship between Islam the religion and Islamism the political ideology on UK campuses. There is minority support (15%) amongst Muslim students generally for the view that they are bound up together. However, active ISOC members were more likely to hold a firm view on the issue, while non-ISOC members were almost three times more likely to be unsure.

Diagram 11: Islam and Politics: Which if any of the following statements comes closer to your view? A comparison of active ISOC members and non-members

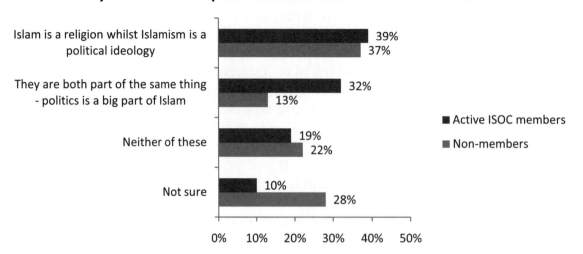

■ *Understandings of Islam: a generational divide*

Muslim students were asked how different their perception of Islam is compared to that of their parents. A third of Muslim students polled (33%) felt their understanding of Islam was to some degree different to that of their parents; 11% felt they had a very different understanding of Islam to that of their parents and just over a fifth of Muslim students (22%) felt their understanding was fairly different. Female Muslim students (14%) were over twice as likely as males (6%) to think their understanding was very different.

By contrast, over half (58%) of Muslim students polled did not feel their understanding was significantly different to that of their parents –three in ten (30%) respondents said 'not very different', 9% said 'not at all different' and 19% said 'it's about the same.'

Diagram 12: How different would you say your perception of Islam is compared to that of your parents?

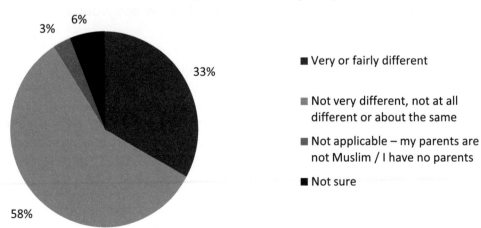

Of the one third of Muslim students polled who said they understood Islam differently to how their parents perceived it, nearly three quarters (72%) said their parents were more "strict"; 39% felt their parents were much more strict Muslims than they are and a third (33%) felt their parents were slightly more so. Nearly a fifth (18%) of those who noted a generational difference felt their parents were more "liberal" Muslims than they are.

Diagram 13: And how would you describe that difference?

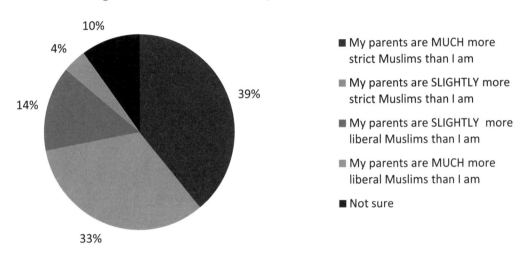

Of those respondents who felt their parents' perception of Islam was different to their own, nearly half of male Muslim students (45%) compared to just over a third (36%) of females said their parents were much more strict than they are. 18% of respondents said their parents' perception of Islam was more liberal than theirs. Female Muslim students (17%) were nearly twice as likely as males (9%) to feel their parents were slightly more liberal than they are. Almost one in fifteen (7%) males believes their parents are much more liberal compared to only one in a hundred females. Overall, male Muslim students were more likely to feel a notable difference from their parents whereas females were more likely to feel a slight difference.

Diagram 14: And how would you describe that difference? A comparison of male and female Muslim students

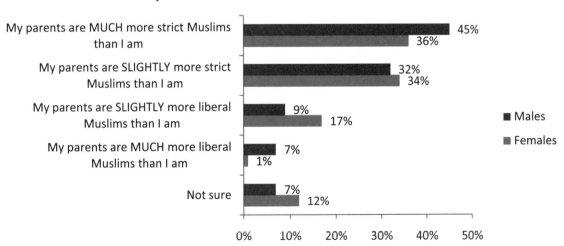

Interpreting Sharia

Sharia, or Islamic principles commonly laid down as legal codes, is derived not only from the Quran, but also from the Hadeeth (recorded sayings and deeds attributed to Mohammed) and from centuries of precedent laid down by diverse – and sometimes competing – Muslim jurists. Questions of interpretation are inevitably fraught with uncertainty.

Poll respondents were asked a series of questions concerning Sharia, aiming to gauge whether they considered Sharia as immutable or open to interpretation. Because of Sharia's centrality to Islam, flexibility on it is arguably evidence of flexibility on the religion as a whole. Activity in an ISOC – and the arguable corresponding familiarity with Islamic doctrine - seems to be the main factor influencing poll respondents' views on Sharia.

■ Interpreting Sharia according to time and place

Muslim students were asked whether they felt it was acceptable for Muslims to want to interpret Sharia according to time and place. A quarter (25%) of Muslim students polled said it was unacceptable for Sharia to be interpreted according to time and place – i.e. that traditional interpretations of Sharia cannot be revised. Almost two-fifths of Muslim students polled (39%), however, said it was acceptable for Sharia to be interpreted according to time and place. Over a third (36%) of respondents said they were not sure – a surprisingly large proportion considering that the interpretation and application of Islamic law are so often discussed in the media.

Diagram 15: Do you think it is generally acceptable or generally unacceptable for Muslims to want to interpret Sharia depending on time and place?

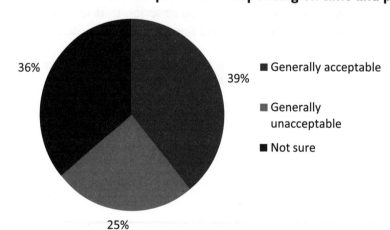

Over half of active ISOC members (53%) thought that Sharia could be revised depending on time and place compared with only a third (35%) of non-ISOC members. Non-ISOC members were twice as likely (39%) as active ISOC members (19%) to be unsure about interpretations of Sharia, suggesting that respondents less engaged with Islam on campus were less likely to form clear opinions about it.

Diagram 16: Do you think it is generally acceptable or generally unacceptable for Muslims to want to interpret Sharia depending on time and place? A comparison of active ISOC members and non-members

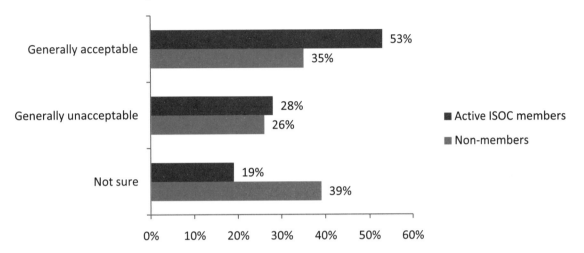

Respondents were then asked if Islam tends to allow such interpretation. Almost a quarter (24%) of respondents said that Islam tends to allow the interpretation of Sharia according to time and place, considerably less than the two fifths (39%) who felt it was acceptable. Fully half of respondents (50%) said they were not sure whether Islam permitted the interpretation of Sharia according to time and place. One in six (16%), however, said that Islam tends to prohibit such an interpretation and one in ten (10%) said the Quran made no reference to it.

Diagram 17: And does Islam tend to allow or tend to prohibit this kind of interpretation?

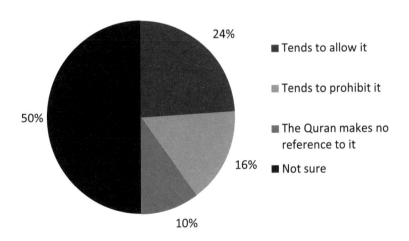

Active ISOC members polled were much more likely than non-members to have formed an opinion on this question – over half of non-members (54%) were unsure as compared to less than a third (31%) of active ISOC members, suggesting a greater engagement with Islam. Active ISOC members were more likely than non-members to believe both that Islam permits the interpretation of Sharia according to time and place (37% and 21% respectively) and that Islam prohibits it (23% and 15% respectively).

Diagram 18: And does Islam tend to allow or tend to prohibit this kind of interpretation? A comparison of active ISOC members and non-members

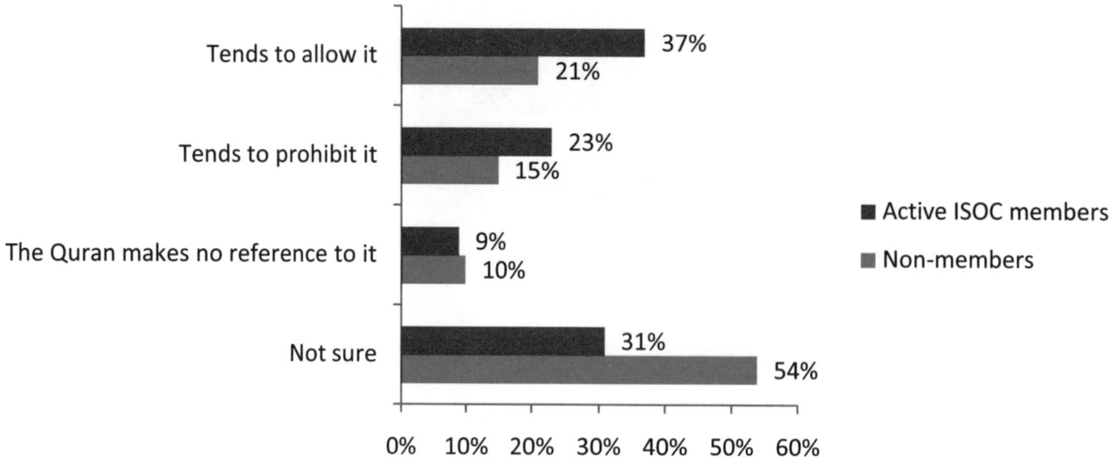

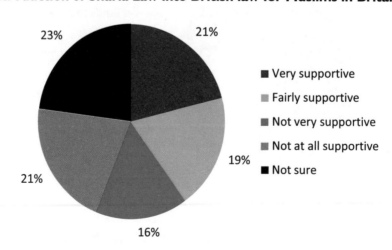

Introducing Sharia to Britain

Muslim students were asked how supportive they would be of the introduction of Sharia Law into British law for Muslims in Britain. Two fifths (40%) of Muslim students polled supported the introduction of Sharia into British law for Muslims – just over a fifth (21%) were very supportive and just under a fifth (19%) were fairly supportive. Slightly fewer (37%) did not support the introduction of Sharia into British law for Muslims – 16% said they were not very supportive whilst over a fifth (21%) said they were not supportive at all. Almost a quarter (23%) said they were not sure.

Diagram 19: How supportive if at all would you be of the official introduction of Sharia Law into British law for Muslims in Britain?

Active ISOC members were much more likely (65%) than non-ISOC members (36%) to support Sharia in Britain. Two fifths (40%) of active ISOC members said they were very supportive of the introduction as compared to one in six (16%) of non-members who said the same. Correspondingly, non-ISOC members were more likely (42%) than active ISOC members (26%) to be unsupportive. Less than one in ten (9%) active ISOC members said they were not supportive at all whilst a quarter (25%) of non-members agreed.

Diagram 20: How supportive if at all would you be of the official introduction of Sharia Law into British law for Muslims in Britain? A comparison of active ISOC members and non-members

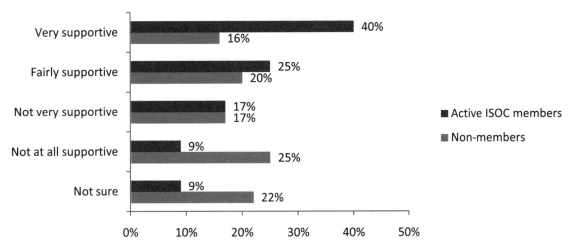

Non-Muslim students polled were even less enthusiastic about the introduction of Sharia into British law: over three quarters (76%) of non-Muslim respondents said they did not support it (61% of all respondents said not at all), 20% were unsure, leaving only 4% fairly supportive and 0% very supportive.

Diagram 21: How supportive if at all would you be of the official introduction of Sharia Law into British law for Muslims in Britain? A comparison of Muslim and non-Muslim students

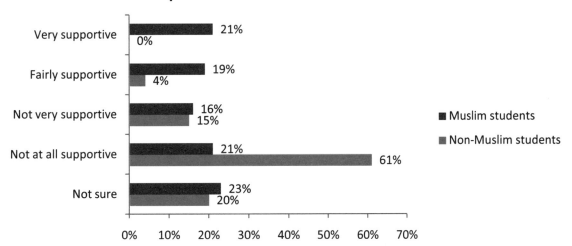

■ *Support for the Caliphate*

Muslim students were asked how supportive, if at all, they would be of the introduction of a worldwide Caliphate based on Sharia Law. The question of erecting a worldwide Caliphate or Islamic state revealed significant polarisation among Muslim students. While arguably few Muslims today consider the rise of such a Caliphate a realistic possibility, many radical groups and movements such as al-Qaeda, Hizb ut-Tahrir and the Muslim Brotherhood openly advocate re-creating a worldwide Caliphate based on Sharia law. A third (33%) of respondents declared themselves supportive of such a Caliphate – over one in six (15%) were very supportive and nearly a fifth (18%) were fairly supportive. A quarter (25%) were unsupportive and over four in ten (42%) unsure.

Diagram 22: How supportive if at all would you be of the introduction of a worldwide Caliphate based on Sharia Law?

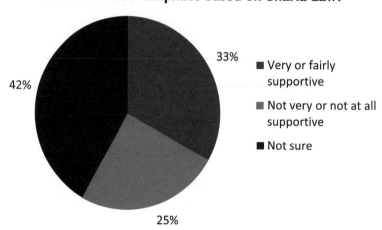

33% ■ Very or fairly supportive

■ Not very or not at all supportive

■ Not sure

42%

25%

As with other questions relating to Sharia, ISOC activity seemed the principle factor affecting respondents' ability to form an opinion and in some cases encouraging them to adopt more radical beliefs.

Diagram 23: How supportive if at all would you be of the introduction of a worldwide Caliphate based on Sharia Law? A comparison of active ISOC members and non-members

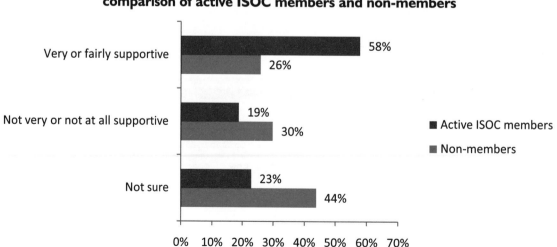

Very or fairly supportive — 58%, 26%

Not very or not at all supportive — 19%, 30%

Not sure — 23%, 44%

■ Active ISOC members
■ Non-members

0% 10% 20% 30% 40% 50% 60% 70%

A majority of active ISOC members polled (58%) said they supported the introduction of a worldwide Caliphate – a third (32%) said they were very supportive and a quarter (26%) fairly supportive. By contrast, only a quarter (26%) of non-ISOC members declared their support. Correspondingly, nearly half (44%) of non-ISOC members polled were unsure, compared with less than a quarter (23%) of active ISOC members.

■ *Killing for the Faith*

Respondents were asked if it is ever justifiable to kill in the name of religion. Just under a third of Muslim students polled (32%) said killing in the name of religion was justified – the vast majority of these (28% of all respondents) said killing could be justified if the religion was under attack and 4% of respondents supported killing in order to promote and preserve that religion. A further one in six (15%) Muslim students polled were unsure leaving just over half (53%) who believe killing in the name of religion was never justifiable.

By contrast, 2% of non-Muslims polled felt killing in the name of religion was justified and a further 4% were unsure. An overwhelming majority – 94% – said killing in the name of religion was never justifiable.

Diagram 24: Is it ever justifiable to kill in the name of religion? A comparison of Muslim student and Non-Muslim student responses

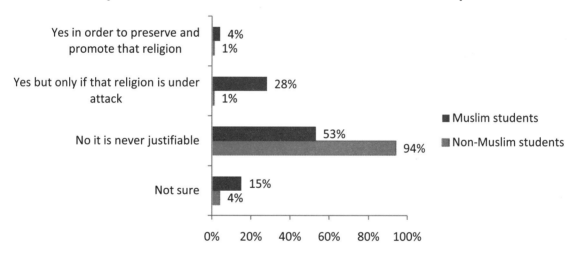

Activity in an ISOC affected results. Three fifths (60%) of active ISOC members polled said they believed it acceptable to kill in the name of religion – one in ten (11%) felt it acceptable to kill in order to promote and preserve that religion and nearly half (49%) said it was acceptable only if that religion was under attack. By contrast, 63% of non-ISOC members said it was never acceptable. Unusually the percentages of active ISOC members and non-members who said they were unsure were roughly equal (10% and 12% respectively), suggesting that on this issue – unlike questions regarding Sharia – non-ISOC members are more likely to form clear opinions.

Diagram 25: Is it ever justifiable to kill in the name of religion? A comparison of active ISOC members and non-members

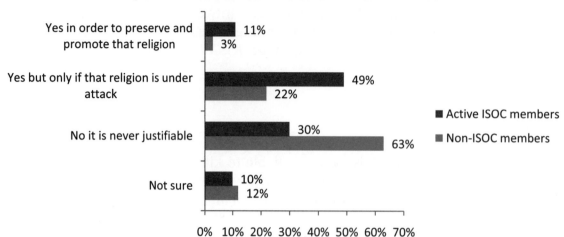

The majority (60%) of active ISOC members believe that it is justifiable to kill in the name of religion as compared to only 2% of non-Muslim students who feel the same. 94% of non-Muslim students said it is never justifiable to kill in the name of religion whilst less than a third (30%) of active ISOC members agreed.

Diagram 26: Is it ever justifiable to kill in the name of religion? A comparison of active ISOC member and non-Muslim students

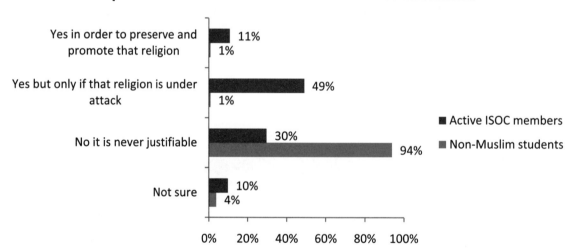

Age was a factor in opinion-forming: younger (age 18-34) respondents were twice as likely (33%) as older (age 35-54) (16%) to support killing in the name of religion. No older (age 35-54) respondents supported killing in order to preserve and promote that religion whilst 70% said it was never justifiable.

Diagram 27: Is it ever justifiable to kill in the name of religion? A comparison of younger (age 18-34) and older (age 35-54) Muslim students

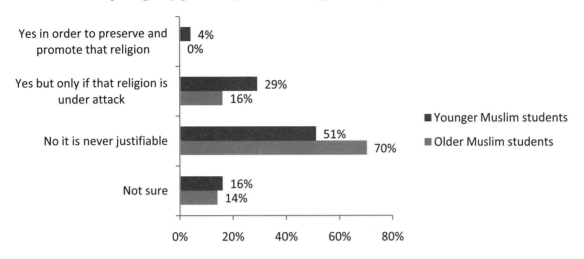

Male Muslim students polled were more likely (35%) than females (28%) to support killing in the name of religion. Females were similarly much more likely (59%) than males (46%) to say that killing in the name of religion was never justifiable and less likely to be unsure.

Diagram 28: Is it ever justifiable to kill in the name of religion? A comparison of male and female Muslim students

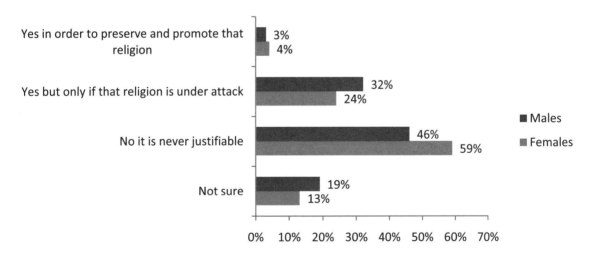

Overall, findings indicate that younger (age 18-34) male active ISOC members are more likely than other Muslim students to support killing in the name of religion, while support is much lower among non-ISOC members, females and older (age 35-54) students.

Opinions shifted slightly when Muslim students were then asked whether geography – i.e. where killing in the name of religion would take place - might affect their thinking. Islamic scripture and tradition often draws a clear distinction between the Muslim and non-Muslim worlds, sometimes with differing behaviour prescribed in each. With regard to violence, the major distinction is usually whether Muslims are engaged in offensive or defensive combat.

A quarter of respondents (27%) said that geography would influence their thinking on violence in religion's name. Over half (56%) of respondents said geography would make no difference, and 17% were unsure.

Diagram 29: Would geography make a difference to your previous answer? [Muslim students only]

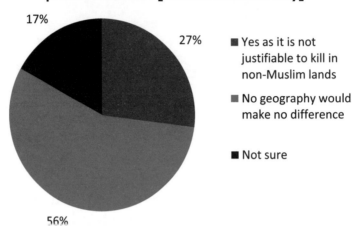

17%

27%

■ Yes as it is not justifiable to kill in non-Muslim lands

■ No geography would make no difference

■ Not sure

56%

■ *Apostasy*

Half (50%) of Muslim students polled said they would not be supportive of a friend's decision to leave Islam. A quarter (25%) said they would be supportive, while another quarter (25%) were unsure. Active ISOC members were more likely (58%) than non-ISOC members (47%) to be unsupportive of a friend's decision to leave Islam, and non-ISOC members more likely (25%) than active ISOC members (14%) to be unsure. Postgraduate students polled were more likely (31%) than undergraduates (23%) to be supportive of a friend's decision to leave Islam whilst female Muslim students polled were slightly more likely (53%) than males (47%) to be unsupportive.

Diagram 30: How supportive if at all would you be if a Muslim friend of yours decided they wanted to leave Islam?

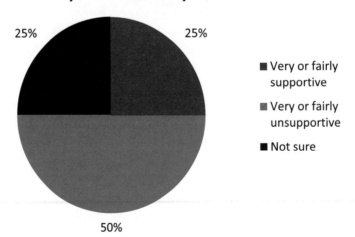

25%

25%

■ Very or fairly supportive

■ Very or fairly unsupportive

■ Not sure

50%

Respondents were then asked what they felt should happen to Muslim apostates. Just over half of the respondents (51%) advocated action of some kind – persuasion or punishment – in response to someone deciding to leave Islam.

Almost half (45%) of Muslim students polled said that apostates should be encouraged to reconsider their decision by Muslim elders and people that care about them. A minority (6%) said that apostates should be punished in accordance with Sharia – males were twice as likely (8%) as females (4%) to hold this view.

Just over a third (36%) of all respondents felt that nothing should happen to apostates – older (age 35-54) students were more likely (42%) than younger (age 18-34) students (35%) to advocate this view. One in eight (13%) respondents were unsure.

Diagram 31: What should happen to a person who decides to leave Islam?

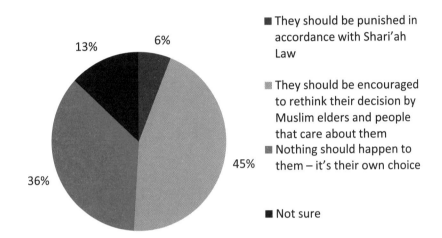

Active ISOC members tended more than other respondents towards a strict view of apostasy and what should happen to a person who decides to leave Islam. One in six (16%) active ISOC members advocated punishing apostates in accordance with Sharia, and a further three fifths (61%) said that apostates should be encouraged to reconsider their decision. By contrast, two fifths (41%) of non-ISOC members said that apostates should be left alone.

Diagram 32: What should happen to a person who decides to leave Islam? A comparison of active ISOC members and non-members

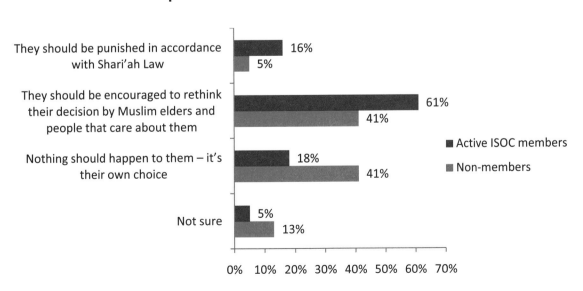

Of the 6% of total respondents who advocated punishing apostates in accordance with Sharia, half (50%) said that they understood this to mean apostates should be killed, a third (34%) said this was not their understanding and 16% were unsure. 3% of Muslim students polled, therefore, felt that apostasy is punishable by death.

Diagram 33: Is it your understanding of Sharia Law that a person who leaves Islam should be killed? [only those who specified 'punished in accordance with Sharia']

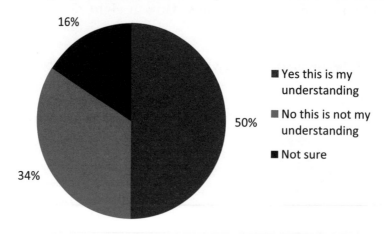

16%

50%

34%

■ Yes this is my understanding

■ No this is not my understanding

■ Not sure

Views on other Muslims

The largest divide in the Muslim world is that between the majority Sunni sect and the minority Shias, which dates to the years immediately following the death of Mohammad, when his followers disagreed over the succession of leadership of the Muslim community.[64] To gauge feelings of sectarianism among Muslim students, respondents were asked whether they considered the other group a) not true Muslims, and b) not true followers of the Quran and the Sunnah, or example of an Islamic life as set by Mohammed.

■ What non-Sunnis say about Sunnis

Just over one in six (15%) of non-Sunni[65] students were hostile to the notion that Sunnis are true Muslims and a further 29% were unsure. A small majority of non-Sunni students polled (56%), however, accepted Sunnis as true Muslims.

Diagram 34: Thinking more about different perceptions of Islam, do you agree or disagree with the following statements? Sunni Muslims are not true believers in Islam [non-Sunni only]

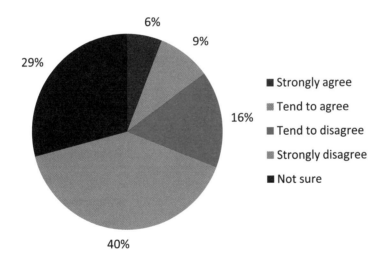

- ■ Strongly agree
- ■ Tend to agree
- ■ Tend to disagree
- ■ Strongly disagree
- ■ Not sure

Responses regarding whether Sunnis followed the Quran and the Sunnah resembled opinions on whether Sunnis were true Muslims. Slightly more non-Sunnis (20%) felt that Sunnis do not follow the Quran and the Sunnah as understood by

---

64 Sunnis and Shias are both guided by the Quran and the hadeeth, but differ on some points of practice. Modern Sunni fundamentalist movements such as Salafism and Wahhabism call for a return to strict Islam as practised during Mohammad's lifetime, sometimes resulting in hostility to perceived deviants such as the Shia and their offshoots.

65 The majority of respodents defined themselves as either Sunni or Shia. However, because several smaller sects were marginally less represented, questions were phrased in terms of "non-Sunni" and "non-Shia".

pious predecessors as they felt Sunnis are not true Muslims and slightly more respondents (35%) were unsure.

**Diagram 35: Sunni Muslims do not follow the Quran and the Sunnah
as understood by the pious predecessors [non-Sunni only]**

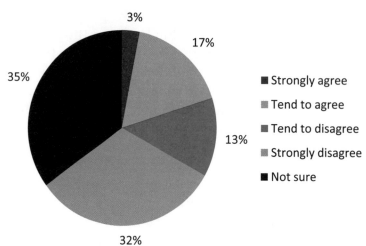

- Strongly agree
- Tend to agree
- Tend to disagree
- Strongly disagree
- Not sure

■ *What non-Shias say about Shias*

Three in ten (30%) non-Shia respondents agreed that Shia Muslims are not true
believers in Islam and just over a quarter (27%) were unsure. Less than half (43%)
of non-Shia respondents said they accepted Shias as true Muslims. Non-Shia males
(33%) were more likely than females (27%) to say that Shia Muslims are not true
believers.

Diagram 36: Shia'a Muslims are not true believers in Islam [non-Shia only]

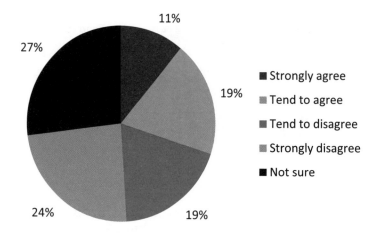

- Strongly agree
- Tend to agree
- Tend to disagree
- Strongly disagree
- Not sure

Almost two fifths (39%) of non-Shia respondents said that Shia Muslims do not
follow the Quran and the Sunnah – a 9% increase on those who felt they are not
true believers in Islam.[66] One in three (30%) disagreed and a further one in three
(31%) were unsure.

---

66 This suggests that some non-Shias may consider Shias nominally Muslim, but not true followers of the Islamic tradition whose guardianship Sunnis believe was passed by Mohammed to one of his leading disciples.
Shias believe that leadership of the Muslim community passed to Mohammed's son-in-law.

Diagram 37: Shia'a Muslims do not follow the Qu'ran and the Sunnah as understood by the pious predecessors [non-Shia'a only]

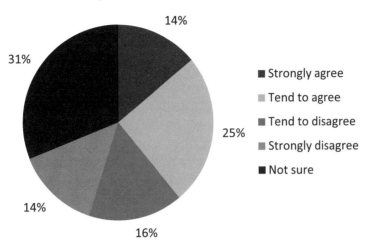

These findings indicate that significant minorities of Sunni and Shia students in the UK do not consider the other sect to be true Muslims and followers of the Quran and the Sunnah. On the other hand, the majority of Muslim students tolerate one another's sectarian differences. Ali al-Mawlawi, a Shia International Studies and Diplomacy postgraduate at SOAS, says:

"I'm used to it to be honest; [sectarianism] is not something that affects me. I get on with my Muslim friends; it's not really a problem to be honest. As long as there's an issue of respect between the two then I don't really see a problem with it."

■ *Sufism*

Muslim students were asked whether they considered Sufism to be based on the Quran and the Sunnah.

Diagram 38: Do you consider Sufism to be…?

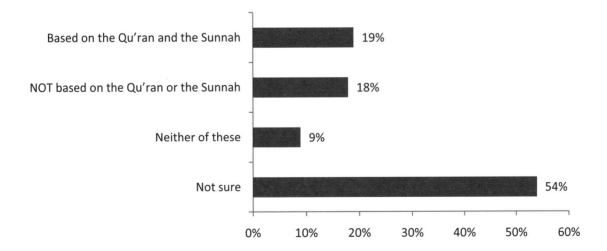

Over half (54%) of Muslim students polled were not sure. Nearly a fifth (19%) of respondents said that Sufism was based on the Quran and the Sunnah and a further fifth (18%) said it was not. Almost one in ten (9%) felt neither statement was accurate.

Active ISOC members were more likely (26%) than non-ISOC members (19%) to consider Sufism to be Quranically sound; but also more likely (28%) than non-ISOC members (17%) to believe the opposite.

Respondents were also asked whether they considered Sufism an ancient Islamic practice or whether they thought that it had developed under Greek and Hindu influences.[67] Again, over half of respondents (53%) were not sure how they would describe Sufism. A fifth of respondents (20%) said it was an ancient Islamic practice, one in ten (10%) said it developed under Greek and Hindu influences, 6% said both and 11% said neither.

Diagram 39: Do you consider Sufism to be...?

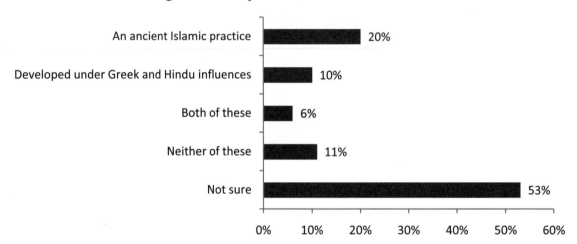

_____

67 Sufism is often called Islamic mysticism. Sufism is not a sect of Islam, it is an approach to Islam aimed at bringing the practioner close to God. Some traditions emphasize poetry, others dance, others meditation and repetitive prayer. At Sufism's core is the concept of dhikr, the constant remembrance and love of God. Many modern Islamic radicals accuse Sufis of corrupting Islam.

Views on Islam and British society

■ *Support for an Islamic political party*

Respondents were asked how supportive, if at all, they would be of the establishment of an Islamic political party to represent the views of Muslims at Parliament in Westminster. Over half of Muslim students polled (54%) were supportive of an Islamic political party to represent the views of Muslims at Parliament – 28% said they were very supportive whilst 26% said they were fairly supportive. Just over a fifth (22%) of Muslim students polled said they were not sure.

Diagram 40: How supportive if at all would you be of the establishment of an Islamic political party to represent the views of Muslims at Parliament in Westminster?

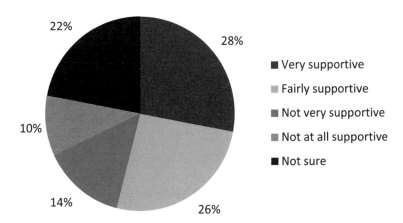

Less than a quarter (24%) of Muslim students polled did not support the establishment of an Islamic political party - 14% said they were not very supportive and one in ten (10%) said they were not supportive at all.By contrast, over half (61%) of non-Muslim students polled did not support the establishment of an Islamic political party.

Active ISOC members (65%) were more likely to be supportive of an Islamic political party in Westminster than non-ISOC members (51%). Fewer active ISOC members were unsupportive: 19% of active ISOC members said they were not very supportive as compared to 15% of non-members. However, non-ISOC members (13%) were over six times more likely than active ISOC members (2%) to say they were not supportive at all. More non-ISOC members (22%) than active ISOC members (14%) were unsure.

Diagram 41: How supportive if at all would you be of the establishment of an Islamic political party to represent the views of Muslims at Parliament in Westminster? A comparison of active ISOC members and non-members

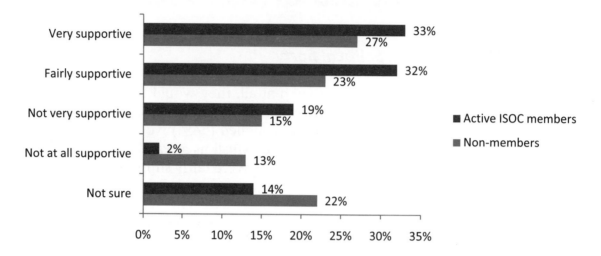

■ *Islam and democracy*

Respondents were asked whether they felt Islam was compatible with the Western notion of democracy. The majority of Muslim students polled (68%) said that Islam is compatible with Western democracy – nearly one in three (29%) felt the two were very compatible whilst almost two fifths (39%) felt they were fairly compatible. 13% said the two were incompatible – 8% said fairly so and 5% said very so. Almost a fifth of respondents (19%) were unsure.

Diagram 42: To what extent if at all do you think Islam is compatible with the Western notion of democracy?

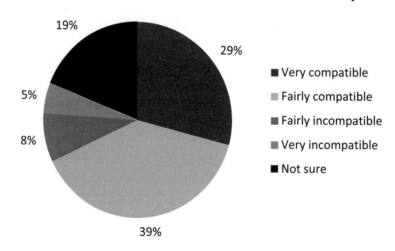

A large majority of active ISOC members (84%) believe that Islam is compatible with the Western notion of democracy, as compared to (64%) of non-ISOC members. Non-ISOC members (21%) were three times more likely than active ISOC members (7%) to be unsure. Older (age 35-54) students were also more likely (78%) than younger (age 18-34) students (67%) to agree that Islam and the Western notion of democracy are compatible.

Diagram 43: To what extent if at all do you think Islam is compatible with the Western notion of democracy? A comparison of active ISOC members and non-members

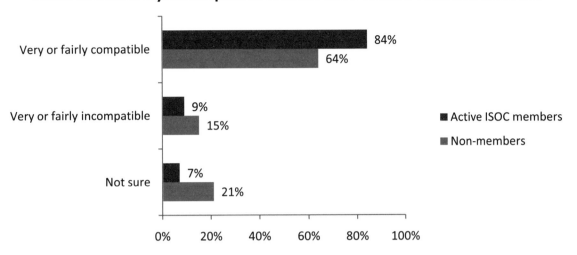

The group most sceptical of Islam's compatibility with the Western notion of democracy are non-Muslim students. In contrast to the majority of Muslim students polled (68%) who said Islam and the Western notion of democracy were compatible, just over a third (34%) of non-Muslim respondents held this view. Half (50%) said that Islam and Western democracy were incompatible and the remainder (16%) were unsure.

Diagram 44: To what extent if at all do you think Islam is compatible with the Western notion of democracy? A comparison of Muslim and non-Muslim students

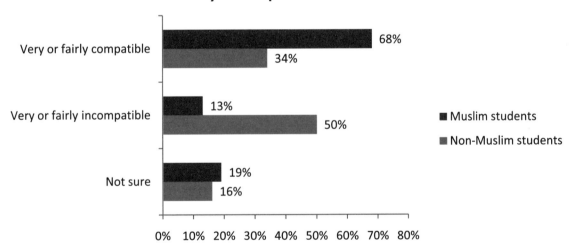

Muslim students polled were thus twice as likely as non-Muslim students to believe that Islam and democracy are compatible, and non-Muslim students polled were almost four times as likely to think the two are incompatible.

■ Islam and secularism

Respondents were then asked if they felt Islam is compatible with the separation of religion and government. Findings indicate divided opinion on the separation of religion and state. Over two fifths (43%) of Muslim students polled said the two were compatible – almost a fifth (18%) felt very so and a quarter (25%) fairly so. Almost three in ten (28%) said they were incompatible – 18% fairly so and one in ten (10%) very so. Almost one in three (29%) – the largest single group – were unsure.

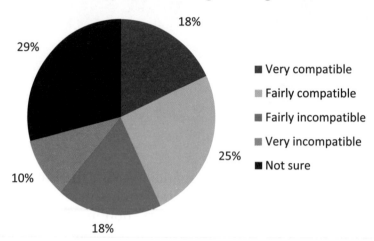

Diagram 45: And how compatible if at all do you think Islam is with the separation of religion and government?

Active ISOC members were much more likely than non-ISOC members to feel that Islam and the separation of religion and government are incompatible: over two fifths (42%) of active ISOC members agreed as compared to a quarter (25%) of non-members. Similar percentages felt Islam and the separation of religion and state were compatible. As a result, almost twice as many non-members (29%) as active members (16%) have yet to form a clear opinion on this issue.

Diagram 46: And how compatible if at all do you think Islam is with the separation of religion and government? A comparison of active ISOC members and non-members

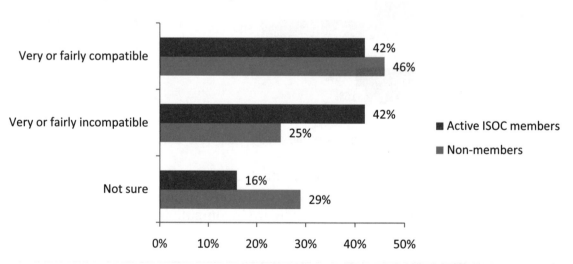

By contrast, over half (55%) of non-Muslim students polled said that Islam and the separation of religion and government were incompatible. A fifth (20%) felt they were compatible and a quarter (25%) were unsure.

Diagram 47: And how compatible if at all do you think Islam is with the separation of religion and government? A comparison of Muslim and non-Muslim students

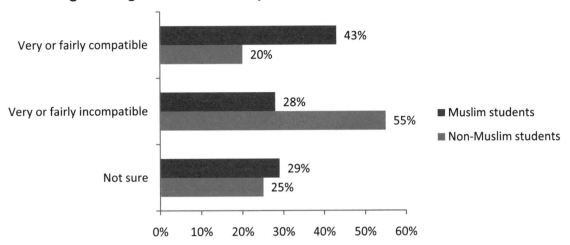

■ **Muslim and British identity**

Muslim students were asked whether they felt it possible to be both Muslim and British equally. A majority of Muslim students polled felt that British and Muslim identities can co-exist: over three quarters of respondents (78%) said that it was possible to be both British and Muslim equally. Others felt it was difficult: 3% said that being British comes first; just over one in eight (12%) said that being Muslim comes first. 7% were unsure.

Diagram 48: Do you think it possible to be both Muslim and British equally?

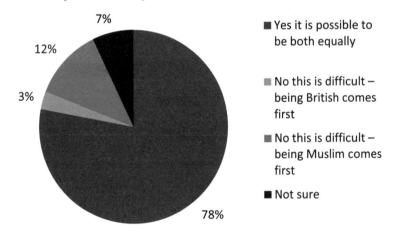

Male Muslim students were more likely than females to feel that being British and Muslim equally is difficult – one in six male (16%) Muslim students said their Muslim identity came first as compared to one in ten (10%) female students who said the same. Correspondingly, female Muslim students (81%) were more likely than males (73%) to say it is possible to be both British and Muslim equally.

Diagram 49: Do you think it possible to be both Muslim and British equally? A comparison of male and female Muslim students

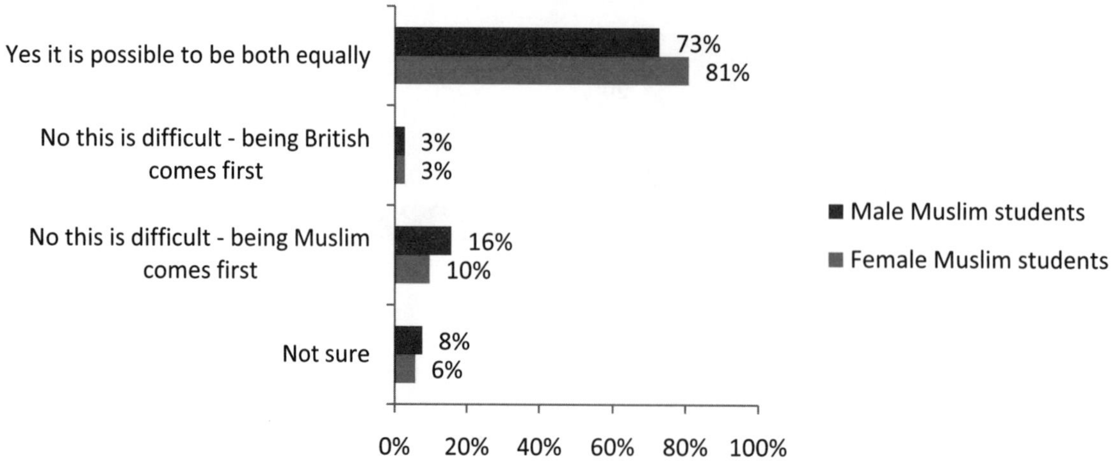

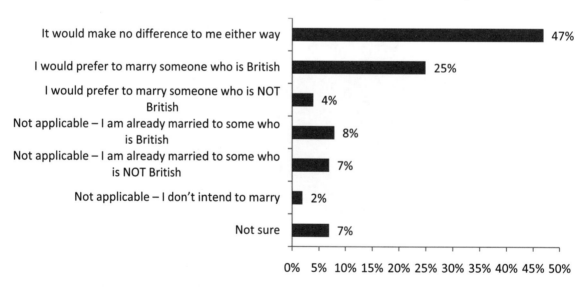

Respondents were also asked whether they would prefer to marry someone British or non-British. Nearly half of respondents (47%) said their spouse's nationality did not matter to them. A quarter (25%) said they would prefer to marry a British person, whilst a small minority (4%) would prefer to marry someone who is not British. More male students (52%) than females (42%) felt that their future spouse's nationality made no difference. Correspondingly, more female students (29%) than males (20%) would prefer to marry someone who is British.

Diagram 50: And thinking about your future, would it be your preference to marry someone who is British someone who is NOT British or would it make no difference to you either way?

Finally, respondents were asked where they hoped to settle and work after completing their studies. Nearly three quarters (70%) planned to stay in the UK. The remaining 30% listed a wide variety of destinations.[68]

---

68 See appendix 1 for a full list of responses to this question.

Respect for others

■ Atheists

Respondents were asked how much respect they had for atheists. Two thirds (66%) of Muslim students polled said they had the same amount of respect for atheists as they had for anyone else. Just over one in ten (11%) Muslim students polled said they had not very much or no respect for atheists and a further 14% were unsure. Almost one in ten (9%) said they had a little or a lot of respect for atheists.

Non-Muslim students polled had slightly more respect for atheists. Over a quarter (28%) said they were atheists; one in ten (10%) had a little or a lot of respect for atheists and over half (56%) said they had the same amount of respect for atheists as they have for anyone else. Only 2% had not very much or no respect and 4% were unsure.

Diagram 51: How much respect do you have for atheists? A comparison of Muslim and non-Muslim students

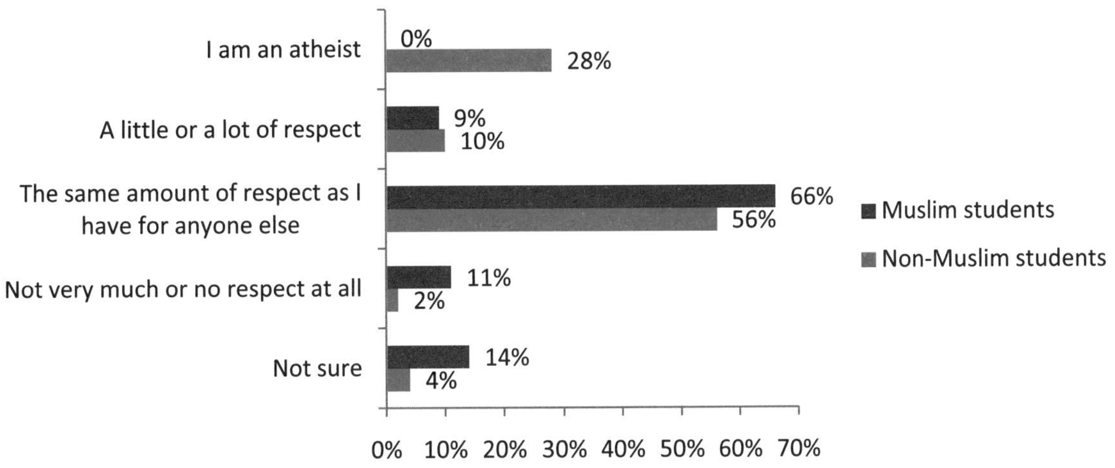

I am an atheist — 0% / 28%
A little or a lot of respect — 9% / 10%
The same amount of respect as I have for anyone else — 66% / 56%
Not very much or no respect at all — 11% / 2%
Not sure — 14% / 4%

■ Muslim students
■ Non-Muslim students

0% 10% 20% 30% 40% 50% 60% 70%

■ Homosexuals

Poll results regarding levels of respect towards homosexuals indicate that Muslim students polled are generally less tolerant of homosexuality than non-Muslims. A quarter (25%) of Muslim students polled said they had not very much or no respect at all for homosexuals and 13% were unsure. Just over half (53%) of Muslim students said they had the same amount of respect as they have for anyone else and almost one in ten (9%) Muslim students said they have a little or a lot of respect for homosexuals.

By contrast, non-Muslim students polled were much more respectful (90%) of homosexuals: 13% said they had a little or a lot of respect for homosexuals; and over three quarters (77%) said they had the same amount of respect as they have for anyone else. 5% are homosexual, 4% said they did not respect homosexuals and only 1% said they were unsure.

Diagram 52: How much respect do you have for homosexuals? A comparison of Muslim and non-Muslim students

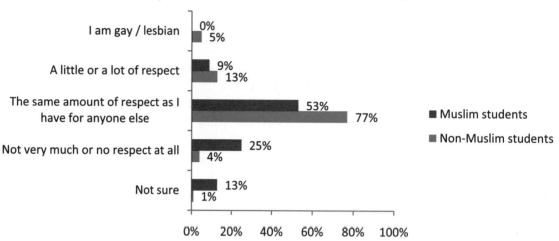

Male Muslim students were the most likely to be intolerant of homosexuality: male Muslim respondents (32%) were much more likely than female Muslim respondents (19%) to have little or no respect for homosexuals. (Amongst non-Muslims polled, the percentages of males and females saying the same were 4% and 3% respectively.) Female Muslim students were more likely than men to display tolerance towards homosexuals: 61% compared to 43% had the same amount of respect as for anyone else.

Diagram 53: How much respect do you have for homosexuals? A comparison of male and female Muslim students

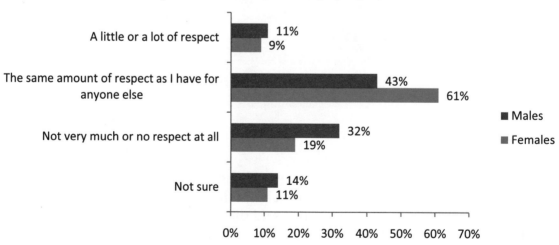

Active ISOC members (20%) were over twice as likely as non-members (9%) to have a little or a lot of respect for homosexuals whilst conversely being more likely than non-ISOC members to have not very much or no respect at all for them (28% compared to 24%).

■ *Jews*

Respondents were also asked how much respect they had for Jews. Almost one in fifteen (7%) Muslim students polled said they had not very much or no respect at all for Jews. Four out of five (79%) Muslim students polled, however, said they respected Jews – almost three fifths (59%) said they had the same amount of respect for Jews as they did for anyone else and a fifth (20%) said they had a little or a lot of respect. A further 14% were unsure.

By contrast, 3% of non-Muslims said they had not very much or no respect at all for Jews. A large majority of non-Muslim students polled (94%) said either that they have the same level of respect for Jews as they have for anyone else (81%) or that they have a little or a lot of respect (13%). 1% said they are Jewish and 2% were unsure.

Diagram 54: How much respect do you have for Jewish people generally? A comparison of Muslim and non-Muslim students

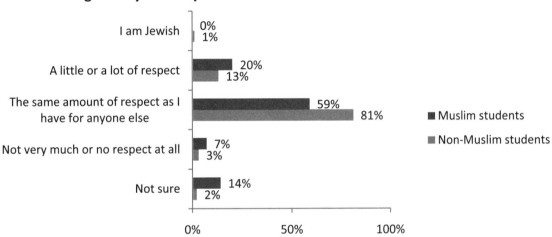

Active ISOC members were slightly more likely (86%) to respect Jews than non-ISOC members (80%). Non-ISOC members (8%) were more likely than active ISOC members (2%) to have not very much or no respect at all for Jews.

Diagram 55: How much respect do you have for Jewish people generally? A comparison of active ISOC members and non-members

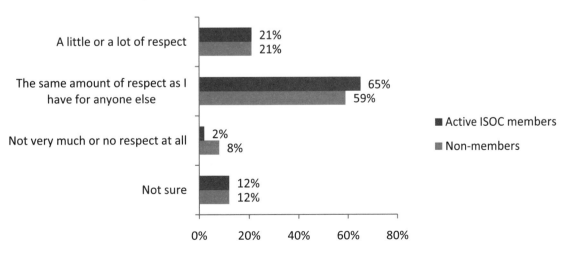

■ *Non-Muslim views on Muslims*

While most questions were directed at Muslim respondents, key questions were also asked of non-Muslim respondents – including how much respect they have for Muslims. Most non-Muslim students (88%) said they had respect for Muslims: three quarters (75%) said they had the same amount of respect for Muslims as they do for anyone else and 13% had a little or a lot of respect for Muslims.

Almost one in ten (9%) non-Muslims polled, however, had little or no respect for Muslims and 3% were unsure. Non-Muslim students polled were therefore more likely to have little or no respect for Muslims (9%) than they were of homosexuals (4%), Jews (3%) or atheists (2%).

Diagram 56: How much respect do you have for Muslims [Non-Muslim students only]

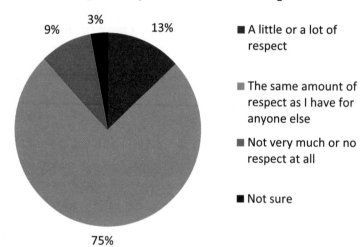

■ A little or a lot of respect

■ The same amount of respect as I have for anyone else

■ Not very much or no respect at all

■ Not sure

Many Muslims students interviewed expressed concern that the wider British public viewed them with undue suspicion. Many mentioned scrutiny by the British media and anti-terrorism legislation introduced in the wake of the 9/11 and 7/7 attacks. Muna Mohamed, recently head sister of the LSE ISOC, says:

> "Me and my friends went to [the London restaurant] Tinseltown at the beginning of my second year and we were sitting there reading a newspaper, and an article was all about 'extremism, campuses, Islamic societies'. And I said, 'My gosh, I'm part of the ISOC and I know the ins and outs of ISOCs and I know that none of what they're saying is true.' So I was really wondering where this negativity comes from."

Some worried that media coverage of extremism encourages the general public to conflate all Muslims with extremists. Yusuf, a postgraduate in Contemporary Politics at the LSE, says:

> "I think actually privileging [extremist] rhetoric in a way, in the media ... actually adds fuel to the fire. Because it makes people within the community sort of frustrated ... If you open up the paper, for example, it's always 'Muslim extremists, Muslim this, Muslim that'. But why does it always have to be qualified as Muslim? I think if you always say 'Muslims this, Muslims this, Muslims this', you're really trying to ... pigeonhole them ... when [extremists] are a very tiny minority of the Muslim community."

Others feel that freedom of speech on campus has been restricted. Amad Ali, an International Studies and Diplomacy postgraduate at SOAS, says:[69]

"I'm not going to get involved with anything dodgy… but for my friends or fellow students I am concerned. You may just say something – 'oh that was really cool that explosion on TV' - and [university authorities] might construe that as, 'Ok, is that what you want to do later when you grow up?'"

---

69 Amad Ali was interviewed on the 28 February, 2008.

Views on women

■ *The Importance of the Hijab*

Muslim students were asked how important it is to Islam that Muslim women wear the hijab. Nearly three fifths (59%) of Muslim students polled felt it was important – half of those felt it was very important and half felt it was very so. Nearly a third (31%) said wearing the hijab was not very or not at all important, and one in ten (10%) were unsure.

Diagram 57: How important to Islam do you think it is that Muslim women wear the hijab?

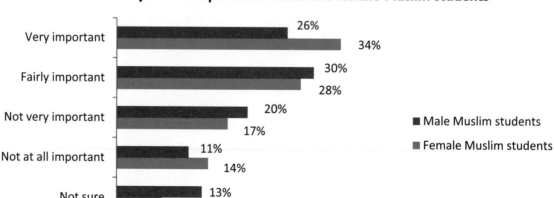

- ■ Very important
- ■ Fairly important
- ■ Not very important
- ■ Not at all important
- ■ Not sure

10%
12%
30%
19%
29%

Percentages were similar between male and female Muslim students – female students, however, had stronger feelings about wearing the hijab than men, being more likely to say it is very important or that it is not at all important.

Diagram 58: How important to Islam do you think it is that Muslim women wear the hijab? A comparison of male and female Muslim students

	Male Muslim students	Female Muslim students
Very important	26%	34%
Fairly important	30%	28%
Not very important	20%	17%
Not at all important	11%	14%
Not sure	13%	7%

Active ISOC members were far more likely (73%) than non-ISOC members (53%) to see wearing the hijab as important – over half (54%) felt it very so and almost a fifth (19%) fairly so. By contrast, a quarter (25%) of non-members felt wearing the hijab was very important and 28% felt it fairly so.

Diagram 59: How important to Islam do you think it is that Muslim women wear the hijab? A comparison of active ISOC members and non-members

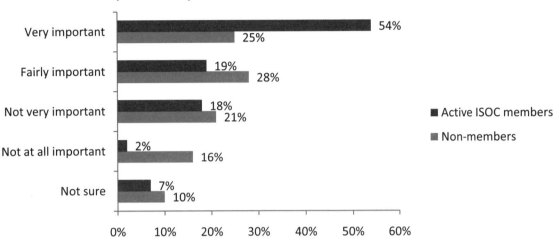

Respondents were also asked whether they felt that "women should wear the hijab – female modesty is an important part of Islam", whether "it is up to the individual Muslim woman as to whether or not she chooses to wear the hijab", or whether they were unsure. In this case, almost a third (31%) of Muslim students polled specified that Muslim females should wear the hijab as a point of Islamic modesty, while just over three fifths (61%) said it should remain a personal choice. Views of men and women varied only slightly.

Diagram 60: Which of the following statements comes closer to you view?

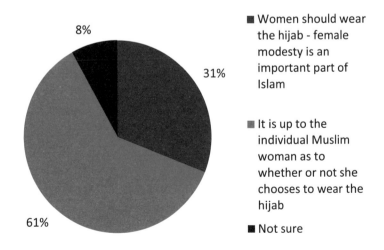

Active ISOC members (51%) were twice as likely as non-members (25%) to say women should wear the hijab – female modesty is an important part of Islam. Just over two fifths (42%) of active ISOC members feel wearing the hijab is a personal choice for Muslim women as compared to two thirds (67%) of non-members.

Diagram 61: Which of the following statements comes closer to you view? A comparison of active ISOC members and non-members.

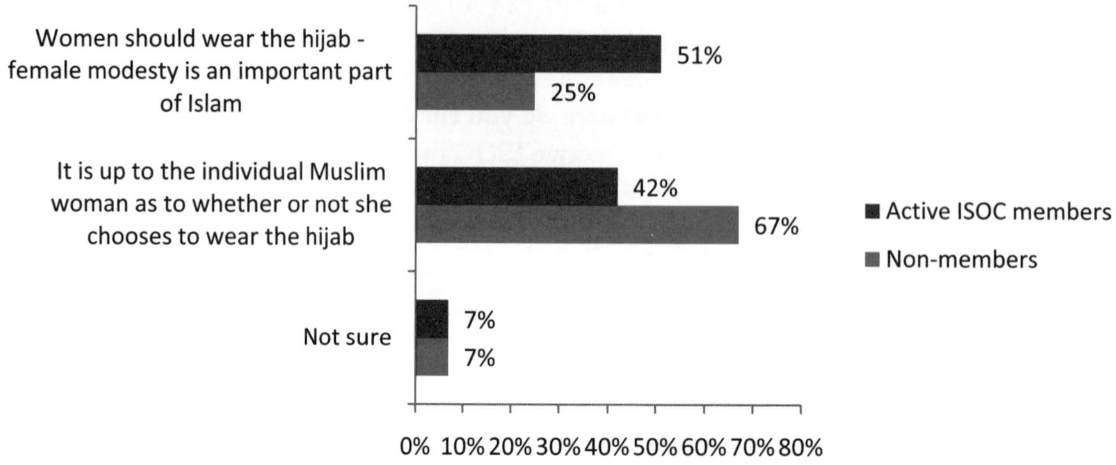

Women should wear the hijab - female modesty is an important part of Islam: 51% Active ISOC members, 25% Non-members

It is up to the individual Muslim woman as to whether or not she chooses to wear the hijab: 42% Active ISOC members, 67% Non-members

Not sure: 7% Active ISOC members, 7% Non-members

■ Active ISOC members
■ Non-members

0% 10% 20% 30% 40% 50% 60% 70% 80%

The tendency of female ISOC members to wear the hijab can create a general impression that not wearing the hijab is frowned upon within the ISOC. Sarah, a 5th-year Medical student at Queen Mary who chooses not to cover her hair, says:[70]

"As with so many things in the society, it's not said but it's felt; it's implied. If I was to walk into a prayer room, or meeting, I would be looked at, and I would be judged. I would feel judged."

Nasima, a 3rd-year Maths student at Queen Mary, says of women who don't wear the hijab:[71]

"I generally do think some people will judge her because she doesn't wear a headscarf. I might wear a headscarf but even then some people will look at me and go 'oh, she wears western clothing'. Having said that, there are some people who generally don't care."

■ *Equality in the eyes of Allah*

Respondents were asked whether they thought men and women are considered equal in the eyes of Allah. 69% of Muslim students polled said that the sexes are equal in the eyes of Allah. Nearly a fifth (17%) felt they are equal in the eyes of Allah except for on one or two issues. One in twenty (5%) said no not really and 2% said no not at all. Less than a quarter (24%) of respondents, therefore, do not feel that men and women are equal in the eyes of Allah, and a further 7% were unsure.

---

70 Sarah was interviewed on the 16 January, 2008.

71 Nasima was interviewed on the 16 January, 2008.

Diagram 62: From your understanding of Islam are men and women considered equal in the eyes of Allah?

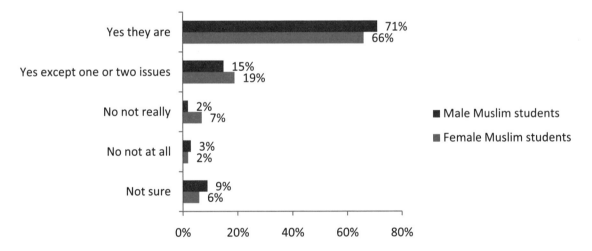

- 7%
- 2%
- 5%
- 17%
- 69%

- ■ Yes they are
- ■ Yes except one or two issues
- ■ No not really
- ■ No not at all
- ■ Not sure

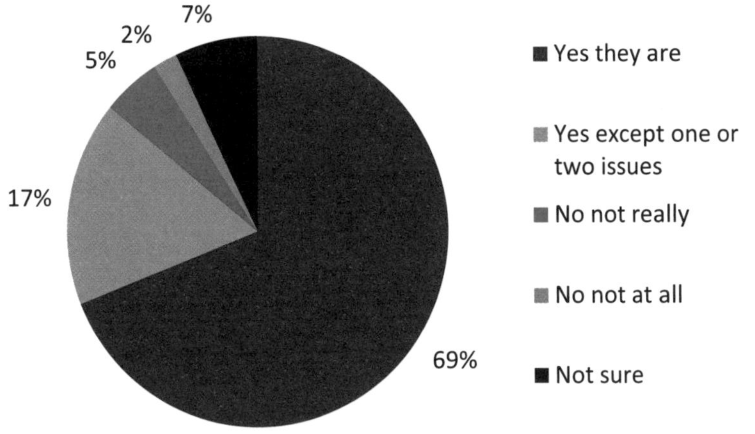

Gender affected the results: female Muslim students were slightly more likely than males to believe that they are not equal to men in the eyes of Allah. Two thirds of female students (66%) felt fully equal to men in the eyes of Allah as compared to 71% of male students who felt the sexes are equal. One in five (20%) of male students did not believe men and women are equal in the eyes of Allah whereas over a quarter (28%) of female students felt the same.

Diagram 63: From your understanding of Islam are men and women considered equal in the eyes of Allah? A comparison of male and female students

	Male Muslim students	Female Muslim students
Yes they are	71%	66%
Yes except one or two issues	15%	19%
No not really	2%	7%
No not at all	3%	2%
Not sure	9%	6%

67

All older (age 35-54) Muslim students (100%) felt that men and woman were either equal or equal except on one or two issues as compared to 84% of younger (age 18-34) Muslim students.

Diagram 64: From your understanding of Islam are men and women considered equal in the eyes of Allah? A comparison of younger (age 18-34) and older (age 35-54) students

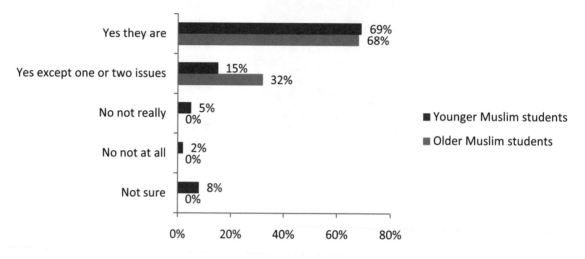

By contrast, an overwhelming majority (76%) of non-Muslims did not feel that men and women are fully equal in the eyes of Allah – a quarter said no not at all (25%), 36% said no not really and just over a sixth (15%) said yes except on one or two issues. Just over one in ten (11%) non-Muslim respondents felt men and women were equal, and 13% were unsure.

Diagram 65: From your understanding of Islam are men and women considered equal in the eyes of Allah? [Non-Muslim students only]

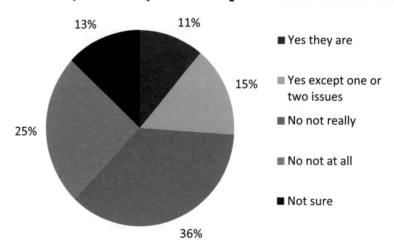

■ *Equality in Britain*

Respondents were then asked whether they felt that males and females were treated equally in their own communities. Less than a third (31%) said that this was the case, just over a quarter (27%) said treatment was equal except on one or two issues, and a third (33%) said males and females were not treated equally. 9% were unsure.

Diagram 66: And in your experience of Islam in your local community are men and women treated equally?

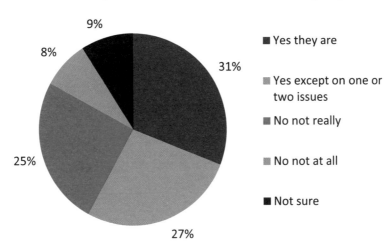

- ■ Yes they are
- ■ Yes except on one or two issues
- ■ No not really
- ■ No not at all
- ■ Not sure

Just over a third (37%) of male Muslim students felt men and women were treated equally in their local communities as compared to just over a quarter (26%) of females who felt the same. Female students (38%) were also more likely than males (27%) to say that women are not really or not treated equally at all in their local communities. In general, female respondents were more likely than males to perceive unequal treatment.

Diagram 67: And in your experience of Islam in your local community are men and women treated equally? A comparison of male and female Muslim students

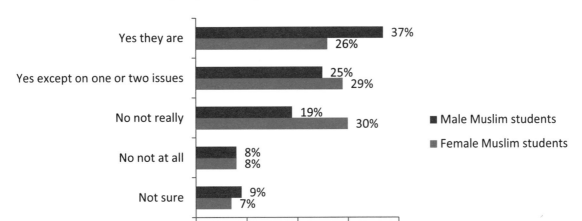

Non-ISOC members were also more likely than active ISOC members to perceive inequality in their local communities. A third (36%) of non-ISOC members felt men and women were not really or not treated equally at all as compared to a fifth (21%) of active ISOC members who said the same. Just over a quarter of (26%) non-ISOC members felt that men and women were treated equally except on one or two issues whilst nearly two fifths (39%) of active ISOC members agreed.

69

Diagram 68: And in your experience of Islam in your local community are men and women treated equally? A comparison of active ISOC members and non-members

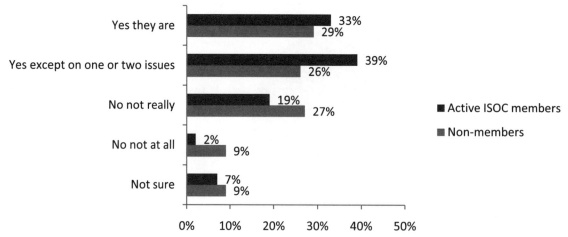

Non-Muslim students were asked whether in their experience of British society Muslim men and women are treated equally. The majority (56%) felt that they were not – four in ten said no not really and 16% said no not at all. Just under a quarter (23%) said they were equal except on one or two issues. Less than one in ten (9%) non-Muslim respondents felt that Muslim men and women were treated unconditionally equally and a further 12% were unsure.

Diagram 69: And in your experience of British society are Muslim men and women treated equally [Non-Muslim students only]

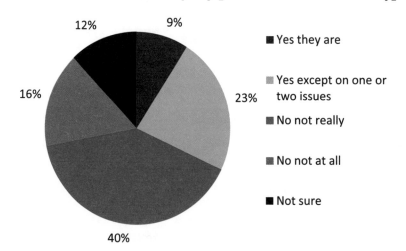

Respondents were also asked whether man and women should be treated equally. Nearly nine out of ten Muslim students polled (89%) said that males and females should be treated equally. One in twenty (5%) said they should not and 6% were unsure.

Diagram 70: Do you believe that men and women *should* be treated equally?

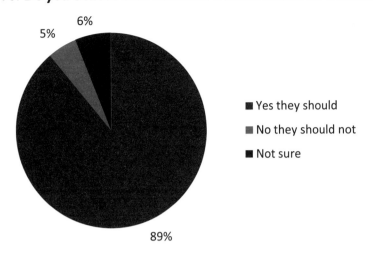

Legend:
- Yes they should
- No they should not
- Not sure

6%
5%
89%

In most ISOCs visited Friday Prayers are segregated, as is traditional in many Islamic cultures, with female students often sitting in a separate room to male students and listening to the *khutba* through loudspeakers. However, some ISOCs, such as Queen Mary, enforce some degree of gender segregation at events, particularly talks, at which women sit at the back and may be obliged to submit handwritten questions while men are free to speak when called upon.

More conservative ISOCs say that segregation does not necessarily imply inequality. Faisal Hanjra, president of Queen Mary ISOC and media spokesman for the FOSIS, says:

> "At Queen Mary, it is quite conservative, in so far as that in a lecture, where there's men and women, there will likely be segregation. Women have to have one entrance, men have one entrance. But what we try and do simultaneously is ensure that there is first of all, democratically, there's women representation in the running of the Islamic society, there's adequate facilities provided for the Muslim women etc ... What we try and do is ensure there's equality between the two."

However, some say this separation has led to inequality with female ISOC members feeling intimidated by their male counterparts. Nasima, a 3rd-year Maths student at Queen Mary, says:

> "It's the simplest things. Asking the brothers for an extra cushion, or asking them for a bottle of water to break our fast, turns into something long winded and complicated ... It's like literally, where you'd be able to go knock on the door and say, 'Hey, can I borrow a bottle of water', it's not quite like that ... For some reason it's always one of the more ... actively involved sisters who goes and asks the brothers for things because ... the ones who aren't as actively involved feel more intimidated by brothers."

Whilst the equal treatment of men and women received majority support from both active ISOC members (86%) and non-members (91%), active ISOC members were over three times more likely (11%) than non-members (3%) to say that men and women should not be treated equally.

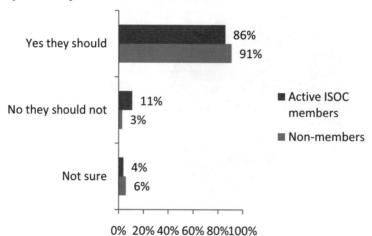

Diagram 71: Do you believe that men and women *should* be treated equally? A comparison of active ISOC members and non-members

■ *"Free mixing"*

Just under half of Muslim students polled (48%) felt that it was acceptable to some extent for Muslim men and women to associate freely – what many British Muslims term "free mixing" – in Muslim society. Four in ten (40%), however, felt it was unacceptable – three in ten (30%) felt that men and women associating freely in Muslim society is not very acceptable and one in ten (10%) said it was not at all acceptable. A further 12% were unsure.

The same numbers of male and female Muslim students – just under half (48%) in both cases – felt that it was acceptable to some extent for men and women to associate freely in Muslim society. More women, however, feel it is unacceptable – 44% compared to 36% – whereas more men (17%) than women (9%) are unsure.

Diagram 72: In your understanding how acceptable is it for men and women to associate freely in Muslim society?

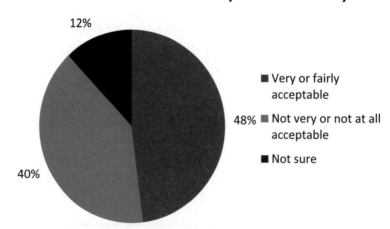

Younger (age 18-34) Muslim students tended to be more liberal than older (age 35-54) students in their views on "free-mixing": older (age 35-54) Muslim students (50%) were slightly more likely than younger (age 18-34) Muslim students (40%)

to feel that men and women associating freely in Muslim society is unacceptable. Active ISOC members and non-members opinions were similar.

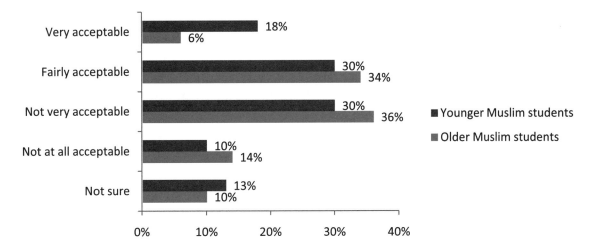

Diagram 73: In your understanding how acceptable is it for men and women to associate freely in Muslim society? A comparison of younger (age 18-34) and older (age 35-54) students.

University life obliges contact between the sexes. Some Muslim students, therefore, differentiate between studying and socialising. Ali al-Mawlawi, an International Studies and Diplomacy postgraduate, says:

"I personally don't mix with female colleagues, socially. At an academic level we have to work together, and that's fine, I don't have a problem with that. Socially I tend to stick with just my male friends."

Comparing traditional Islamic conduct with life as a Muslim in a secular Western country like Britain can be challenging for Muslim students in the UK. Junaid, a 3rd year Maths student at Queen Mary, says:

"In the times of our beloved prophet … the women would be segregated away from the men, and men were segregated away from women at all times. Then someone's changed stuff to get implemented, then you start losing the true ways, and they're not doing nothing wrong [sic] at all. Absolutely not doing nothing wrong … But me, on the other example, an individual, I don't know whether I'm doing wrong or whether I'm doing right … I was born into society like this, I was born into integration, and men and women integrate, so it's time that I commit [and] decide not to integrate with women full stop."

Views of foreign affairs

■ *The war in Iraq*

Respondents were asked whether Britain's foreign policy had affected their respect for the British government, and whether the British public's reaction to that policy had affected their respect for British society. The results indicate that the British government has lost popularity among British Muslim students, as well as among non-Muslim students.

Two thirds of Muslim students polled (66%) said they had lost respect for the British government owing to the war in Iraq. In comparison, fewer non-Muslim students polled (53%) agreed. Nearly a fifth of Muslim students polled (18%) recorded no change in their respect for the British government, as compared to just over a third (34%) of non-Muslim students. 14% of Muslim respondents and 11% of non-Muslims were unsure. Only 2% of Muslim and non-Muslim respondents said their respect for the government had increased.

Diagram 74: How has Britain's involvement with the war in Iraq affected the amount of respect you have for the British government? A comparison of Muslim and non-Muslim students

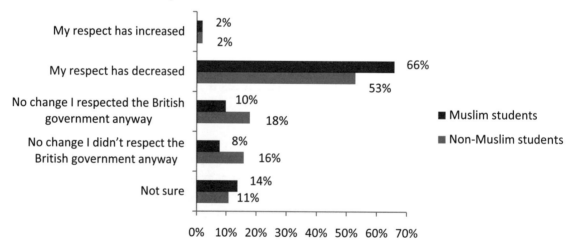

Poll respondents respected the British public's reaction to the war in Iraq more than they respected the government's involvement in the war. Nearly a third (30%) of Muslim students polled said their respect for British society had increased based on the public's (largely negative) reaction to recent government policy, while only 20% said their respect for the British society had decreased. Non-Muslim respondents displayed similar – though less dramatic – shifts in opinion.

Diagram 75: And how has the British public's reaction to the war in Iraq affected the amount of respect you have for British society? A comparison of Muslim and non-Muslim students

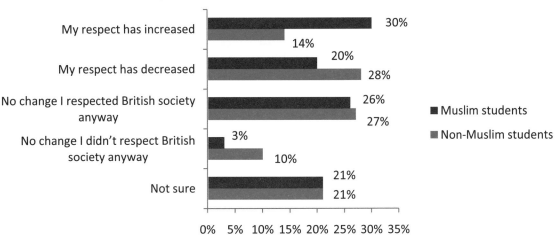

The views of ISOC members differed only slightly from non-members' opinions.

■ *Muslim soldiers in the British armed forces*

Respondents were asked whether they felt that British Muslim servicemen should be allowed to opt out of taking part in military operations in Muslim countries. A majority (57%) of Muslim students polled said that they should – over a third (36%) strongly agreed and a further fifth (21%) tended to agree. Just under a fifth of Muslim students in the UK (18%) disagreed and a quarter of all respondents (25%) were unsure.

Diagram 76: To what extent to do you agree or disagree that Muslims serving in the British armed forces should have the right to opt out of the army if they are required to fight in Muslim countries?

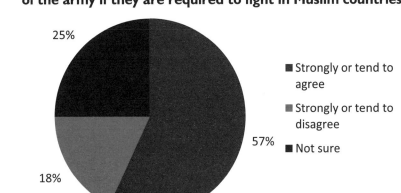

ISOC activity affected Muslim respondents' opinions dramatically. Three quarters (75%) of active ISOC members were in favour of an opt-out for Muslim servicemen fighting in Muslim countries – over half (52%) strongly agreed and a further 23% tended to agree with the suggestion. 16% were unsure and fewer than one in ten (9%) were against an opt-out – 5% tended to disagree and 4% strongly disagreed.

Diagram 77: To what extent to do you agree or disagree that Muslims serving in the British armed forces should have the right to opt out of the army if they are required to fight in Muslim countries? A comparison of active ISOC members and non-member

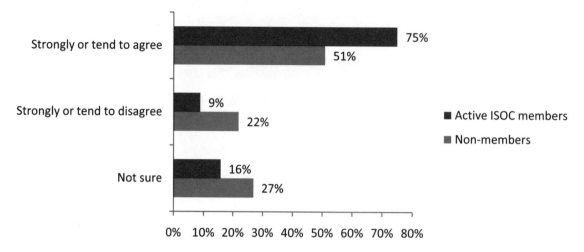

In contrast to Muslim students polled, a large majority (71%) of non-Muslim respondents said that Muslim servicemen should *not* be allowed to opt out of serving in Muslim lands – 42% strongly disagreed with the suggestion of an opt-out and a further 29% tended to disagree. Less than a fifth (18%) of non-Muslim respondents said that Muslim servicemen should be allowed the option (3% strongly agreed and 15% tended to agree). Just over one in ten (11%) were unsure.

Diagram 78: To what extent to do you agree or disagree that Muslims serving in the British armed forces should have the right to opt out of the army if they are required to fight in Muslim countries? A comparison of Muslim and non-Muslim students

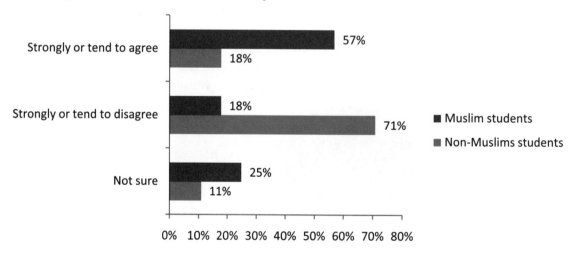

Respondents were then asked whether non-Muslims in the British armed forces should be allowed to opt out of serving in certain areas. Responses closely mirrored those regarding an opt-out for Muslim servicemen amongst Muslim and non-Muslim students polled.

Diagram 79: And to what extent do you agree or disagree that non-Muslims serving in the British armed forces should have the right to opt out of the army if they are required to fight in certain areas? A comparison of Muslim and non-Muslim students

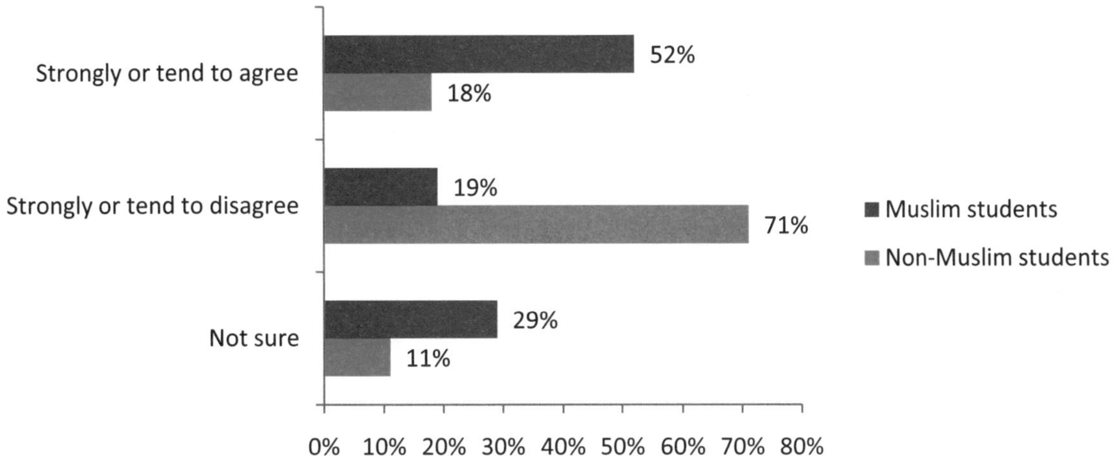

Strongly or tend to agree — Muslim students 52%, Non-Muslim students 18%

Strongly or tend to disagree — Muslim students 19%, Non-Muslim students 71%

Not sure — Muslim students 29%, Non-Muslim students 11%

■ Muslim students
■ Non-Muslim students

0% 10% 20% 30% 40% 50% 60% 70% 80%

■ *Judaism and Zionism*

Respondents were asked how similar they felt Judaism and Zionism were. Nearly half of Muslim students polled (45%) said they were not sure. Less than a third (31%) said they were not similar – 16% said not very and 15% said not at all. Just under a quarter (24%) said the two were similar – 18% said fairly and 6% said very so.

Diagram 80: How similar do you consider the concepts of Judaism and Zionism to be?

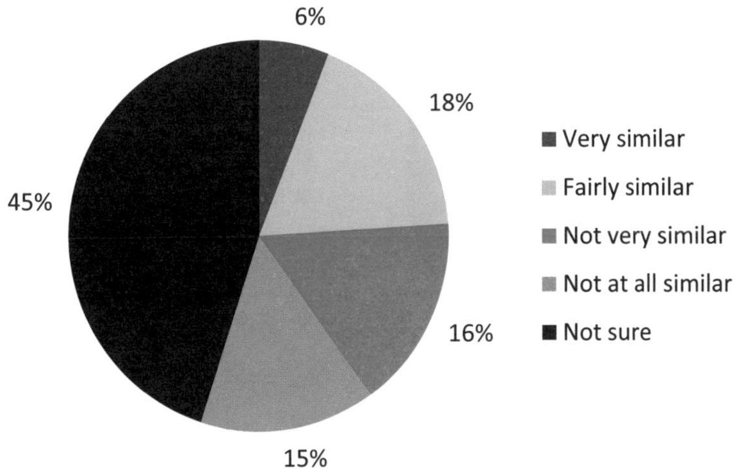

6%
18%
45%
16%
15%

■ Very similar
■ Fairly similar
■ Not very similar
■ Not at all similar
■ Not sure

Active ISOC members were more likely (26%) than non-ISOC members (22%) to conflate Judaism and Zionism, but also more likely (37%) than non-ISOC members (31%) to say the two were not similar. Non-ISOC members, by contrast, were more likely (47%) than active members (37%) to be unsure.

77

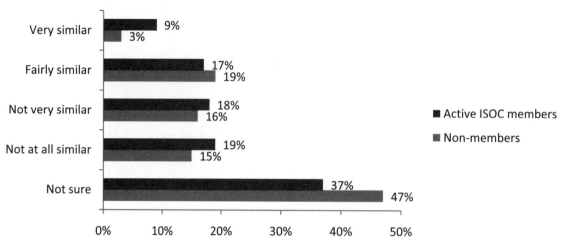

Diagram 81: How similar do you consider the concepts of Judaism and Zionism to be? A comparison of active ISOC members and non-members

Respondents were then asked if they agreed that Judaism is a religion whilst Zionism is a political ideology or whether they felt they were both part of the same thing. Just over a third (34%) of Muslim students polled said that Judaism is a religion and Zionism a political ideology. Just over one in seven (13%) said they were the same thing – Judaism and Zionist politics are fundamentally entwined. 6% felt neither of these statements were accurate and almost half (47%) were unsure.

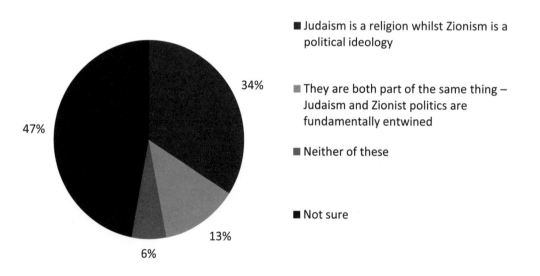

Diagram 82: Which of the following statements comes closer to your view?

The Israeli –Palestine conflict can lead some Muslims to conflate Judaism with Zionism. Yusuf, a Contemporary Politics postgraduate at the LSE, says:

"You can … draw a distinction between Jews and Israelis. Unfortunately I think a lot of the Muslim world groups them together, a lot of Muslims in general, they say … that all Muslims hate Jews or something like this, because they just associate all [Jews] with Israelis. Certainly you can't deny that some of the crimes the Israelis has committed in the name of [Israel's] security, they have violated human rights, and Human Rights Watch and all these organisations, and the UN, have cited this, and they have to evaluate these issues."

Active ISOC members (40%) were again more likely than non-members (32%) to distinguish between the two and more likely to say the two are part of the same thing – 18% and 12% respectively. Non-ISOC members were most likely to be unsure.

Diagram 83: Which of the following statements comes closer to your view? A comparison of active ISOC members and non-members

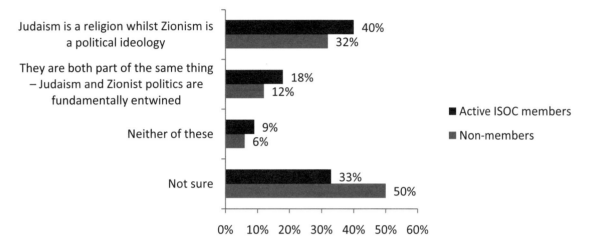

Summary

Poll results indicate that respondents' understandings of Islam and how this affects their outlook more generally is significantly affected by their level of activity in their university's ISOC, their gender and age.

■ *Activity in ISOCs*

Active membership in ISOCs appeared to have a significant effect on the religious beliefs, social networks and overall worldview of Muslim students polled, as well as their attitudes toward non-Muslims, women and minorities. These trends suggest that ISOCs may play a considerable role in shaping the ideas and opinions of their active members. Active ISOC members make up just over a tenth of Muslim students in the UK.

Active ISOC members polled were more likely to be religiously observant on campus, being three times more likely than non-ISOC members polled to always attend Friday prayers. Half of active ISOC members polled visited the prayer-room more than once a day, compared to only 12 percent of non-members. They were also more likely to say that ISOCs are "an important voice" for Muslim students, compared to non-members, who did not rate ISOCs' importance so highly.

In addition to being more religiously observant on campus, active ISOC members polled were also more likely to subscribe to Islamist beliefs, being nearly three times likelier than non-members to say that Islam and Islamism are "part of the same thing". Active members were also nearly twice as likely to support the introduction of the Sharia into British law and more than twice as likely to support the introduction of "a worldwide caliphate based on Sharia law". They were also twice as likely as non-ISOC members polled to think that wearing a hijab is "very important" and more likely to believe that men and women should not be treated equally. Active ISOC members polled were also more likely to support religious violence; active ISOC members were more than twice as likely as non-members to say that "it is justifiable to kill in the name of religion" and half as likely as non-members polled to believe that such killing is "never justifiable". They were also three times more likely to believe that Muslims who decide to leave Islam "should be punished according to Sharia law."

Active ISOC members polled were more likely than other Muslim students to say that Islamic scriptures could be re-interpreted to changing political circumstances and to say that Islam and democracy were "compatible". At the same time, however, active ISOC members' tendencies to reject secularism strongly suggest that this does not equate to a belief in western-style, secular and democratic politics. For example, active ISOC members polled were more likely than other Muslim students to support the establishment of an Islamic political party, with only 2 per-cent of active ISOC members opposing the idea, while also being 17 percent more likely to believe that Islam was incompatible with secularism. Also, 75 percent of active ISOC members believed that Muslims in the British army should be allowed to opt out of conflicts in Muslim countries, compared to 52 percent of non-ISOC members.

Active ISOC members polled were also more likely than other Muslim students to have fixed views on a wide range of issues and less likely to say that they were unsure. In some cases, this seemed to lead to active ISOC members having strongly polarised views. For example, active ISOC members were more likely than non-ISOC members to consider Sufism to be based on the Quran but also more likely than non-ISOC members to believe the opposite. Similarly, active ISOC members were over twice as likely as non-members to have a little or no respect at all for homosexuals whilst conversely being more likely than non-ISOC members to have not very much or no respect at all. Active ISOC members were also less likely to perceive sexual discrimination than non-members, being more likely to believe that men and women were treated equally in their "local community".

Overall, poll results suggest that active ISOC members are likely to be more opin-ionated on issues relating to Islam and Muslims, but at the same time more in-tolerant of others, more dogmatic in their views and less likely to perceive sexual discrimination. Active ISOC membership may tend to heighten individuals' aware-ness of differences between themselves and wider society. For example, while only 5 percent of non-ISOC members say that "most of my friends are Muslims because I have more in common with them", for active ISOC members this figure is 25 percent. However, without further research, it is difficult to say whether more con-servative individuals generally are attracted to ISOCs, where they often go on to become the society's leading members, or whether the teachings of ISOCs generally encourage and promote such attitudes in their followers.

■ *Gender*

Female Muslim students polled were generally less outwardly religiously observ-ant than men but also, on some issues, more supportive of conservative teachings regarding issues such as the hijab and "free-mixing" between men and women. At the same time, however, women polled were more likely than men to perceive sexual inequality in the treatment of men and women, as well as being more likely than men to say that they were "not sure" on issues and less likely to be strident on issues such as homosexuality and killing in the name of the faith.

Female Muslim students polled said they attended Friday prayers less than men. Only 15 percent of women said they always attended Friday prayer, compared to 39 percent of men. Similarly, 44 percent of women said they never attended Friday prayer, compared to 8 percent of men. However, this does not necessarily indicate that women are less religious or observant than men, as in many Islamic cultures women do not regularly or habitually attend communal Friday prayers at mosques. Indeed, women are just as likely as men to be active members of an ISOC.

Female Muslim students polled were generally less supportive of violence than male Muslim students polled: 28 percent of Muslim women said that killing in the name of religion was justified compared to 35 percent of men. Similarly, women were 15 percent more likely than men to say that such killing was never justified. Women were also half as likely as men to say that Muslim apostates "should be punished in accordance with the Sharia". Furthermore, Sunni women were also less likely than men to say that Shia Muslims were not true Muslims, while Muslim women as a whole were also less likely to be intolerant of homosexuality than Muslim men.

On issues relating to sexual equality, women's interpretation of their religion also diverged sharply from those of men polled. For example, female students polled were 5 percent less likely than men to think that men and women were "equal in the eyes of Allah" and comparably more likely than men to believe that men and women were not equal in the eyes of Allah – although it is unclear whether they were supportive or unsupportive of this perceived inequality. Similarly, female Muslim students were more likely than men to say that men and women were not treated equally in their "local community".

Separately, more women than men believed that wearing the hijab was "important". However, Muslim women polled were simultaneously more likely than men to say that wearing the hijab was "not at all important". Similarly, more women than men were opposed to "free-mixing" between men and women in Muslim society: 44 percent of women felt such free-association was unacceptable compared to 36 percent of men. Significantly, men were twice as likely as women to be "not sure" on this issue. On most other issues, women were more likely than men to be undecided.

■ Age

The poll indicates that "younger" (18-34) and "older" (35-54) Muslim students often have significantly different understandings of Islam. In general, the younger generation appear to be more conservative than older students and more supportive of Islamist ideologies. These views are especially prevalent in areas such as killing in the name of religion, apostasy, the compatibility of Islam with Western democracy and the equality of women.

One of the largest divides between older and younger Muslim students polled emerged over the issue of whether religious violence is "ever justifiable". A third of younger Muslim students polled believed that killing in the name of religion could be justified, in contrast with older Muslim students, only 16 percent of whom agree. In addition, while no older Muslim students polled believed killing to be justifiable "in order to preserve and promote the religion", 4 percent of younger students did. A similar generational gap seems to exist on the issue of apostasy, with younger students polled less tolerant than older Muslims towards those who leave the Islamic faith.

Older and younger Muslim students polled also differed on how to interpret the

Quran with regards to the equality of women. No older Muslim students polled believed that men and women were not considered equal ('no, not really' and 'no, not at all') in the eyes of Allah, yet 7 percent of younger students believed that such an inequality existed, with a further 8 percent unsure. Older students were also less likely to think that it was "very important" for women to wear the hijab and more likely to think that men and women should be treated equally. However, the trend of younger Muslim students being more conservative was reversed regarding "free-mixing" between the sexes. Half of older Muslim students polled regarded such free-mixing as unacceptable, as opposed to 40% of younger students.

There are other indications that younger Muslim students are less likely to find common ground between the West and Islam. A third of younger Muslim students polled said that Islam was incompatible with Western notions of democracy, compared with 78 percent of older students who believed that they were. Similarly, older students were more likely to believe that "it is possible to be both Muslim and British equally" and less likely to believe that reconciling these identities was "difficult". Older Muslim students were also less likely to support the establishment of a Caliphate while being almost 20 percent more inclined to believe that Islam was compatible with "the separation of religion and government".

A comparable generational divide is also apparent between Muslim students and their parents. A third of Muslim students polled said that they perceived their religion differently from their parents; with nearly a fifth of those saying that their parents were more "liberal" than they were and nearly three quarters saying they were more "strict". This is in contrast to the majority of the poll results, which show younger Muslims tending to be more conservative than their elders.

Conclusion

This report shows that British Muslim students hold a diverse and broad range of opinions. The majority of Muslim students have tolerant ideas towards other minorities, reject violence in the name of their faith and support Britain's secular and democratic society as well as its system of governance.

However, there are also reasons for concern. Significant minorities of Muslim students – and particularly younger ones – support violence in the name of Islam, endorse punishing Muslim apostates "in accordance with the Sharia" and believe that men and women are not equal in the eyes of Allah and should not be treated equally. Comparable minorities, around 10 percent of Muslim students, also have little or no respect for Jews, atheists or homosexuals and support Islamist proposals such as re-creating the Caliphate, introducing Sharia law to Britain and establishing an Islamic political party. Sizable numbers, between 20 and 30 percent of Muslim students, also hold intolerant attitudes towards minority forms of Islam such as Shi'ism and Sufism.

The report additionally suggests that active members of Islamic Societies are more likely than other Muslim students to hold such intolerant views – notwithstanding that active ISOC members are also more likely to believe that democracy and re-interpreting the Sharia are compatible with Islam. ISOC leaders and former members make up the membership of the Federation of Student Islamic Societies (FOSIS). However, as only a minority of Muslim students are active members of ISOCs, FOSIS' claims to represent British Muslim students should be treated with caution. Treating FOSIS as representative of all Muslim students risks disproportionately empowering a small number of highly conservative, and sometimes Islamist, individuals at the expense of ordinary Muslims.

At the same time, a significant minority of non-Muslims polled had a hostile view of Islam, being less respectful towards Muslims than towards other minorities such as Jews, homosexuals and atheists. Non-Muslims are also more likely to believe that the narrow and intolerant interpretations of Islam promoted by Islamist and conservative groups represent the "true" Islam: for example, more than half of non-Muslims polled believe that Islam favours inequitable treatment of women and is incompatible with secularism. This strongly suggests that Islamist groups and the ideas they promote are partly responsible for the intolerance found on campuses towards Muslim students and their religion.

The poll results also indicate that a large proportion of Muslim students, up to 40 percent depending on the question, are undecided on key issues such as the legitimacy of religious violence, respecting others and whether Islam is compatible with secularism. Many of these individuals could either be won over to intolerant Islamist ideologies or to secular, democratic understandings of Islam. Which path these swing voters take will be crucial in deciding the future of British Islam.

The government, university authorities and Muslims themselves need to do three things to ensure that pluralistic Muslim voices triumph. They need to take action to diminish Islamist influence on campus, engage Muslims not yet committed to any specific interpretation of Islam, and support and strengthen the many Muslim groups and individuals who are already convinced that Islam is a democratic and progressive force for good.

Glossary*

Dajjal: the false Messiah, or anti-Christ, whose appearance marks the imminent end of the world. The Arabic root means "to deceive, cheat, take in."

Da'wah: inviting or calling people to Islam, proselytizing.

Hijab: traditionally means a partition which separates two things i.e. a curtain. In modern times it is used to describe a form of women's dress, specifically the covering of the head.

Iftar: the evening meal breaking the daily fast during the Islamic holy month of Ramadan.

Jihad: lit. "struggle". It is usually defined in a religious sense as a "struggle in the path of Allah". Interpretations range from a personal effort to live according to Islam or inner struggle against the self, to defence or propagation of Islam by arms or physical fighting. For the latter, Islam traditionally believes that human communities have the right to collective self-defence.

Khutba: a speech, and in particular a standing speech given by the Imam before the *Jumu'a* prayer and after the two *Eid* (Muslim holidays) prayers.

Masjid: mosque, place of worship.

Niqab: veil that covers the entire face of a woman.

Quran: Islamic Holy Book, a collection of revelations from Allah to Muhammad via the angel Gabriel. The revelation began in 610AD to 632AD. The original text is in Arabic.

Sahaba: the Companions of the Prophet Muhammad, as well as people who have seen Muhammad at least once.

Salafi: (*Salaf*), lit. meaning righteous predecessors; Salafism is a movement which takes early generations of Muslims, often the first three generations after Muhammad, as examples of how Islam should be followed. Salafis (pl.) idealize an uncorrupted, pure Islamic religious community.

Shia: lit. a part or faction, specifically the party who claim that Ali should have succeeded Muhammad as the first Caliph (leader of the Muslim community).

Sharia: lit. road, the legal modality of a people based on the Revelation of their Prophet. The final *Sharia* is that of Islam. Sharia is based on Islamic principles of jurisprudence, which ranges from diverse traditions and interpretations of strict rules to broad principles and objectives.

Sunnah: the customary practice of a person or group of people. It has come to refer almost exclusively to the practice of Muhammad and to the first generation of Muslims.

Sunni: the main body of Muslims, the *Ahl as-Sunna wa'l-Jama'a*, who recognise and accept the *Khulafa' ar-Rashidun*, the first four Caliphs.

Wahhabism: used to describe an Islamic revivalist movement which sprang up in the Arabian peninsula in the 18th century, founded by Muhammad Ibn Abdul-Wahhab. This interpretation is heavily based on Salafism (see *Salafi*).

Wahhabi: a member of a sect dominant in Arabia. Earlier followers supported the family of Sa'ud and helped bring the Ottoman Caliphate to an end.

* Definitions are mostly taken from Aisha Bewley's 'Glossary of Islamic Terms', 1998, Ta-Ha Publishers

APPENDIX 1:

Muslim students poll results

YouGov / Centre for Social Cohesion Survey Results*
Sample Size: 632
Fieldwork: 22nd January - 14th February 2008

Centre for Social Cohesion	Total	Male	Female	18-34	35-54	Active in ISOC	Non-ISOC Member
All Muslim students	**632**	297	335	579	48	72	411
	%	%	%	%	%	%	%
Do you follow any of the three main Abrahamic religions?							
Yes Christianity	**0**	0	0	0	0	0	0
Yes Islam	**100**	100	100	100	100	100	100
Yes Judaism	**0**	0	0	0	0	0	0
No I follow another religion	**0**	0	0	0	0	0	0
No I do not follow any religion	**0**	0	0	0	0	0	0
Which branch of Islam do you follow?							
Sunni	**79**	82	78	79	80	81	78
Shia'a	**9**	10	8	10	4	16	9
Ahmadiyya	**2**	1	3	2	6	0	2
Alawi	**0**	0	0	0	0	0	0
Ismaili	**2**	2	1	2	0	2	2
Other	**8**	5	10	8	10	2	9
Are you a member of your university's Islamic Society?							
Yes	**25**	24	25	26	12	100	0
No	**65**	64	66	63	82	0	100
Not applicable – my university doesn't have an Islamic Society	**10**	12	9	11	6	0	0
And how active would you say you are in the Islamic Society? [only those in Islamic Society]							
I'm a committee member of my Islamic Society	**8**	7	9	8	0	18	0
Very active – I go to all of the meetings and events	**10**	12	9	11	0	23	0
Fairly active – I go to most of the meetings and events	**27**	25	29	28	17	60	0
Not very active – I go to some meetings and events but not many	**33**	30	36	33	50	0	0
Not at all active – I'm a member but I never attend meetings or events	**21**	25	17	21	17	0	0
Not sure	**1**	2	0	0	17	0	0

* Figures shown in italics denote findings which are too small to be statistically viable. On some occasions figures shown here will differ by 1% to those in part two where the raw results have been rounded up or down where appropriate.

Centre for Social Cohesion	Total	Male	Female	18-34	35-54	Active in ISOC	Non-ISOC Member
All Muslim students	**632**	297	335	579	48	72	411
	%	%	%	%	%	%	%

From what you know about your university's Islamic Society, which, if any, of the following statements do you generally agree with? [Please tick all that apply.]

	Total	Male	Female	18-34	35-54	Active in ISOC	Non-ISOC Member
The Islamic Society is an important voice for Muslim students at my university	**42**	43	41	43	32	75	36
The Islamic Society is really just a chance for Muslims to get together	**36**	32	39	37	22	28	38
The Islamic Society tends to promote interfaith activities (e.g. between Muslims Jews Hindus and Sikhs etc.)	**34**	35	34	37	16	63	28
Some Muslims within the Islamic Society have very different understandings of Islam	**22**	21	23	23	10	30	21
There is some debate within the Society about the kind of ideas the Islamic Society should promote	**13**	15	12	14	6	32	12
The Islamic Society tends to discourage interfaith activities (i.e. between Muslims Jews Hindus and Sikhs etc.)	**3**	6	2	3	4	4	5
None of these	**22**	21	22	19	44	4	23

Do you tend to think of Islam as a religion or a way of life?

	Total	Male	Female	18-34	35-54	Active in ISOC	Non-ISOC Member
A religion	**13**	13	14	14	14	12	14
A way of life	**30**	33	28	30	26	25	29
Both	**52**	48	55	51	54	63	52
Not sure	**5**	6	4	5	6	0	5

How often, if at all, do you visit the campus prayer room at your university?

	Total	Male	Female	18-34	35-54	Active in ISOC	Non-ISOC Member
At least once a day	**17**	20	15	17	18	51	12
Between two and five times a week	**10**	8	11	10	6	18	6
About once or twice a week	**8**	12	5	8	6	19	5
About once or twice a month	**6**	9	3	6	2	5	6
Less than once a month	**8**	8	8	8	6	5	9
I have never visited the campus prayer room	**35**	27	42	35	38	2	49
Not applicable – my campus doesn't have a prayer room	**16**	15	16	15	24	0	13

And how often, if at all, do you attend Friday prayer?

	Total	Male	Female	18-34	35-54	Active in ISOC	Non-ISOC Member
I always attend Friday prayer	**26**	40	15	26	26	37	23
I nearly always attend Friday prayer	**16**	22	11	15	20	28	13
I occasionally attend Friday prayer	**16**	19	14	18	8	16	16
I rarely attend Friday prayer	**14**	12	16	13	26	11	15
I never attend Friday prayer	**27**	8	44	28	20	9	33

89

Centre for Social Cohesion	Total	Male	Female	18-34	35-54	Active in ISOC	Non-ISOC Member
All Muslim students	**632**	297	335	579	48	72	411
	%	%	%	%	%	%	%

Which, if any, of the following statements comes closer to your view?

Islam is a religion whilst Islamism is a political ideology	**36**	35	36	36	34	39	37
They are both part of the same thing – politics is a big part of Islam	**16**	18	14	15	16	32	13
Neither of these	**22**	21	23	22	26	19	22
Not sure	**27**	26	28	28	24	11	28

How supportive, if at all, would you be of the establishment of an Islamic political party to represent the views of Muslims at Parliament in Westminster?

Very supportive	**28**	32	25	29	30	33	27
Fairly supportive	**26**	24	27	26	24	32	24
Not very supportive	**14**	14	14	14	16	19	15
Not at all supportive	**10**	10	11	9	14	2	13
Not sure	**22**	21	23	23	16	14	22

And how supportive, if at all, would you be of the official introduction of Shari'ah Law into British law for Muslims in Britain?

Very supportive	**21**	22	20	21	20	40	16
Fairly supportive	**19**	16	22	20	20	25	20
Not very supportive	**16**	19	13	16	10	18	17
Not at all supportive	**21**	21	21	20	28	9	25
Not sure	**23**	22	24	23	22	9	23

How different would you say your perception of Islam is compared to that of your parents?

Very different	**11**	6	14	10	14	9	11
Fairly different	**22**	23	22	22	26	23	20
Not very different	**30**	32	28	32	16	37	30
Not at all different	**9**	8	10	8	12	11	10
It's about the same	**19**	18	19	19	16	18	19
Not applicable – my parents are not Muslim / I have no parents	**3**	3	3	2	8	0	4
Not sure	**7**	10	4	7	8	4	6

And how would you describe that difference?
[only those who differed]

My parents are MUCH more strict Muslims than I am	**40**	45	35	40	35	22	43
My parents are SLIGHTLY more strict Muslims than I am	**33**	32	34	34	30	44	34
My parents are SLIGHTLY more liberal Muslims than I am	**14**	9	17	16	0	28	10
My parents are MUCH more liberal Muslims than I am	**4**	7	1	3	10	6	4
Not sure	**10**	7	12	8	25	0	9

Centre for Social Cohesion	Total	Male	Female	18-34	35-54	Active in ISOC	Non-ISOC Member
All Muslim students	**632**	297	335	579	48	72	411
	%	%	%	%	%	%	%

THINKING MORE ABOUT DIFFERENT PERCEPTIONS OF ISLAM, DO YOU AGREE OR DISAGREE WITH THE FOLLOWING STATEMENTS...?

Sunni Muslims are not true believers in Islam
[non-Sunni only]

Strongly agree	**6**	11	2	5	0	18	5
Tend to agree	**9**	16	5	8	20	0	11
Tend to disagree	**16**	21	13	15	30	9	16
Strongly disagree	**40**	39	40	43	10	64	34
Not sure	**29**	14	40	28	40	9	34

Shia'a Muslims are not true believers in Islam
[non-Shia'a only]

Strongly agree	**11**	14	8	12	4	19	9
Tend to agree	**19**	19	19	20	15	21	20
Tend to disagree	**19**	20	19	19	21	23	16
Strongly disagree	**24**	23	25	24	25	27	25
Not sure	**27**	25	29	26	35	10	30

Sunni Muslims do not follow the Qu'ran and the Sunnah as understood by the pious predecessors
[non-Sunni only]

Strongly agree	**3**	7	0	3	0	9	3
Tend to agree	**17**	23	13	17	20	18	19
Tend to disagree	**13**	14	13	12	20	0	15
Strongly disagree	**32**	32	31	34	10	46	28
Not sure	**36**	25	44	35	50	27	35

Shia'a Muslims do not follow the Qu'ran and the Sunnah as understood by the pious predecessors
[non-Shia'a only]

Strongly agree	**14**	19	11	15	10	23	13
Tend to agree	**25**	25	24	25	23	33	22
Tend to disagree	**16**	15	18	16	15	21	17
Strongly disagree	**14**	14	14	14	10	10	15
Not sure	**31**	27	34	30	42	13	33

Do you consider Sufism to be...?

Based on the Qu'ran and the Sunnah	**19**	21	18	18	26	26	19
NOT based on the Qu'ran or the Sunnah	**18**	19	16	18	14	28	17
Neither of these	**9**	10	9	9	10	18	7
Not sure	**54**	50	57	55	50	28	56

Centre for Social Cohesion						Active in ISOC	Non-ISOC Member
	Total	Male	Female	18-34	35-54		
All Muslim students	**632**	297	335	579	48	72	411
	%	%	%	%	%	%	%

Do you consider Sufism to be...?

An ancient Islamic practice	**21**	21	20	19	30	23	22
Developed under Greek and Hindu influences	**10**	12	9	11	6	12	9
Both of these	**6**	7	4	5	10	5	6
Neither of these	**11**	12	10	11	10	25	8
Not sure	**53**	48	57	54	44	35	54

Do you think it is generally acceptable or generally unacceptable for Muslims to want to interpret the Shari'ah depending on time and place?

Generally acceptable	**39**	37	40	39	32	53	35
Generally unacceptable	**25**	24	26	25	28	28	27
Not sure	**36**	39	34	36	40	19	39

And does Islam tend to allow or tend to prohibit this kind of interpretation of the Shari'ah?

Tends to allow it	**24**	27	21	24	22	37	21
Tends to prohibit it	**16**	17	16	17	14	23	15
The Qu'ran makes no reference to it	**10**	9	11	9	14	9	10
Not sure	**50**	47	53	51	50	32	54

Are there any parts of Shari'ah Law (for example punishments like stoning or lashing etc.) that you think should be modernised for use in Britain?

Yes some parts should be modernised for use in Britain	**34**	33	35	34	30	40	35
No Shari'ah Law is sacred and should stay as it is	**32**	36	29	32	38	44	31
Not sure	**34**	31	36	34	32	16	35

And what about Shari'ah Law more generally: should it be modernised for use in places like Saudi Arabia?

Yes Shari'ah Law should be modernised for use in places like Saudi Arabia	**35**	34	35	34	38	30	37
No Shari'ah Law is sacred and should stay as it is in Muslim countries	**38**	40	35	38	38	58	33
Not sure	**28**	26	30	28	24	12	30

To what extent if at all do you consider yourself to be 'British'?

I am British	**62**	63	61	61	62	54	62
I consider myself partially British and partially something else	**21**	16	25	22	14	30	20
I am not British	**12**	14	10	11	20	11	13
Not sure	**5**	7	4	6	4	5	5

Centre for Social Cohesion	Total	Male	Female	18-34	35-54	Active in ISOC	Non-ISOC Member
All Muslim students	**632**	297	335	579	48	72	411
	%	%	%	%	%	%	%

Do you think it possible to be both Muslim and British equally?

Yes it is possible to be both equally	**78**	74	81	77	80	75	78
No this is difficult – being British comes first	**3**	3	3	3	2	5	3
No this is difficult – being Muslim comes first	**12**	16	10	13	10	16	11
Not sure	**7**	8	6	7	8	4	7

And thinking about your future would it be your preference to marry someone who is British, someone who is NOT British, or would it make no difference to you either way?

It would make no difference to me either way	**47**	52	42	48	36	51	48
I would prefer to marry someone who is British	**25**	20	29	26	10	28	22
I would prefer to marry someone who is NOT British	**4**	3	5	4	2	7	4
Not applicable – I am already married to some who is British	**8**	7	9	7	16	4	10
Not applicable – I am already married to some who is NOT British	**7**	6	8	5	26	4	8
Not applicable – I don't intend to marry	**2**	2	3	2	4	2	2
Not sure	**7**	10	5	8	6	5	7

To what extent, if at all, do you think Islam is compatible with the Western notion of democracy?

Very compatible	**29**	34	26	29	26	40	29
Fairly compatible	**39**	37	40	38	52	44	36
Fairly incompatible	**8**	7	10	9	4	7	10
Very incompatible	**5**	6	4	4	6	2	5
Not sure	**19**	17	21	20	12	7	21

And how compatible, if at all, do you think Islam is with the separation of religion and government?

Very compatible	**18**	23	15	17	24	18	20
Fairly compatible	**25**	24	26	24	36	25	26
Fairly incompatible	**18**	14	20	18	18	26	16
Very incompatible	**10**	11	8	10	2	16	10
Not sure	**29**	27	31	30	20	16	29

How supportive, if at all, would you be of the introduction of a worldwide Caliphate based on Shari'ah Law?

Very supportive	**15**	16	15	16	14	32	11
Fairly supportive	**18**	20	16	17	30	26	15
Not very supportive	**12**	11	14	13	10	12	14
Not at all supportive	**13**	15	12	12	20	7	16
Not sure	**41**	39	44	43	26	23	44

Centre for Social Cohesion	Total	Male	Female	18-34	35-54	Active in ISOC	Non-ISOC Member
All Muslim students	632	297	335	579	48	72	411
	%	%	%	%	%	%	%

Thinking about your university friends, which of the following statements comes closest to describing your social group?

	Total	Male	Female	18-34	35-54	Active in ISOC	Non-ISOC Member
Most of my friends at university are Muslim, because I have more in common with them than I do with non-Muslims	**8**	9	7	8	6	25	5
Some of my friends at university are Muslim, but I have friends from all sorts of different backgrounds	**37**	37	38	37	38	53	34
Very few of my friends at university are Muslim; there aren't many Muslims at my university	**4**	3	4	4	2	0	5
Very few of my friends at university are Muslim; I find I have more in common with non-Muslims	**5**	6	6	6	2	0	6
Religion is not an issue when I choose my friends at university	**38**	35	41	37	46	19	42
Not sure	**8**	12	4	8	6	4	7

How supportive, if at all, would you be if a Muslim friend of yours decided they wanted to leave Islam?

	Total	Male	Female	18-34	35-54	Active in ISOC	Non-ISOC Member
Very supportive	**10**	6	13	10	8	12	10
Fairly supportive	**15**	16	15	15	12	16	18
Fairly unsupportive	**22**	19	23	22	24	30	20
Very unsupportive	**29**	28	30	28	32	28	27
Not sure	**25**	31	20	25	24	14	25

What should happen to a person who decides to leave Islam?

	Total	Male	Female	18-34	35-54	Active in ISOC	Non-ISOC Member
They should be punished in accordance with Shari'ah Law	**6**	8	4	6	6	16	5
They should be encouraged to rethink their decision by Muslim elders and people that care about them	**45**	42	48	46	42	61	41
Nothing should happen to them – it's their own choice	**36**	34	39	35	42	18	41
Not sure	**12**	16	10	13	10	5	13

How important to Islam do you think it is that Muslim women wear the hijab?

	Total	Male	Female	18-34	35-54	Active in ISOC	Non-ISOC Member
Very important	**30**	26	34	31	26	54	25
Fairly important	**29**	30	28	28	38	19	28
Not very important	**19**	20	18	19	14	18	22
Not at all important	**12**	11	14	12	14	2	16
Not sure	**10**	13	7	10	8	7	10

Which of the following statements comes closer to your view?

	Total	Male	Female	18-34	35-54	Active in ISOC	Non-ISOC Member
Women should wear the hijab – female modesty is an important part of Islam	**31**	30	31	31	34	51	25
It is up to the individual Muslim woman as to whether or not she chooses to wear the hijab	**61**	58	64	60	64	42	67
Not sure	**8**	12	5	9	2	7	7

Centre for Social Cohesion	Total	Male	Female	18-34	35-54	Active in ISOC	Non-ISOC Member
All Muslim students	**632**	297	335	579	48	72	411
	%	%	%	%	%	%	%
In your understanding, how acceptable is it for men and women to associate freely in Muslim society?							
Very acceptable	**17**	16	18	18	6	19	18
Fairly acceptable	**31**	32	30	30	34	28	31
Not very acceptable	**30**	26	34	30	36	35	29
Not at all acceptable	**10**	10	10	10	14	9	11
Not sure	**12**	17	9	13	10	9	12
From your understanding of Islam, are men and women considered equal in the eyes of Allah?							
Yes they are	**69**	71	67	69	68	68	69
Yes except one or two issues	**17**	15	19	15	32	21	19
No not really	**5**	2	7	5	0	4	5
No not at all	**2**	3	2	2	0	0	2
Not sure	**7**	9	6	8	0	7	6
And in your experience of Islam in your local community, are men and women treated equally?							
Yes they are	**31**	37	26	31	30	33	29
Yes except on one or two issues	**27**	24	29	27	26	39	26
No not really	**25**	19	31	24	36	19	27
No not at all	**8**	8	8	9	4	2	10
Not sure	**9**	11	7	10	4	7	9
Do you believe that men and women should be treated equally?							
Yes they should	**89**	88	91	89	96	86	91
No they should not	**5**	4	5	4	4	11	3
Not sure	**6**	8	4	7	0	4	5
Is it ever justifiable to kill in the name of religion?							
Yes, in order to preserve and promote that religion	**4**	3	4	4	0	11	3
Yes, but only if that religion is under attack	**28**	32	24	29	16	49	22
No, it is never justifiable	**53**	46	59	51	70	30	63
Not sure	**15**	19	13	16	14	11	12
Would geography make a difference to your previous answer?							
Yes as it is not justifiable to kill in non-Muslim lands	**27**	26	27	27	25	38	21
No geography would make no difference	**56**	57	56	57	38	56	63
Not sure	**17**	18	17	17	38	6	16

Centre for Social Cohesion	Total	Male	Female	18-34	35-54	Active in ISOC	Non-ISOC Member
All Muslim students	**632**	297	335	579	48	72	411
	%	%	%	%	%	%	%

To what extent do you agree or disagree that Muslims serving in the British armed forces should have the right to opt out of the army if they are required to fight in Muslim countries?

Strongly agree	**36**	39	33	36	26	53	32
Tend to agree	**21**	20	22	21	24	23	19
Tend to disagree	**9**	8	9	9	4	5	10
Strongly disagree	**10**	10	10	10	12	4	12
Not sure	**25**	24	27	25	34	16	27

And to what extent do you agree or disagree that NON-Muslims serving in the British armed forces should have the right to opt out of the army if they are required to fight in certain areas?

Strongly agree	**29**	32	26	29	24	46	26
Tend to agree	**23**	22	25	24	20	28	22
Tend to disagree	**10**	9	10	9	10	5	11
Strongly disagree	**9**	11	8	8	14	4	11
Not sure	**29**	27	32	29	32	18	30

How has Britain's involvement with the war in Iraq affected the amount of respect you have for the British government?

My respect has increased	**3**	2	3	3	2	7	2
My respect has decreased	**66**	67	64	65	66	67	64
No change: I respected the British government anyway	**10**	9	11	9	18	11	11
No change: I didn't respect the British government anyway	**8**	7	9	9	4	4	9
Not sure	**14**	15	13	15	10	12	14

And how has the British public's reaction to the war in Iraq affected the amount of respect you have for British SOCIETY?

My respect has increased	**30**	32	27	30	26	35	28
My respect has decreased	**20**	20	19	20	10	18	20
No change: I respected British society anyway	**26**	24	28	24	48	26	26
No change: I didn't respect British society anyway	**3**	2	4	4	0	4	4
Not sure	**21**	21	22	22	16	18	22

NOW THINKING ABOUT JUDAISM AND ZIONISM...

How similar do you consider the concepts of Judaism and Zionism to be?

Very similar	**6**	7	4	6	4	9	3
Fairly similar	**18**	14	22	17	24	18	19
Not very similar	**16**	19	13	16	18	18	16
Not at all similar	**15**	19	12	14	20	19	15
Not sure	**45**	41	49	48	34	37	47

Centre for Social Cohesion	Total	Male	Female	18-34	35-54	Active in ISOC	Non-ISOC Member
All Muslim students	**632**	297	335	579	48	72	411
	%	%	%	%	%	%	%
Which of the following statements comes closer to your view?							
Judaism is a religion whilst Zionism is a political ideology	**34**	41	28	33	42	40	32
They are both part of the same thing – Judaism and Zionist politics are fundamentally entwined	**13**	14	13	13	14	18	12
Neither of these	**6**	5	7	6	6	9	6
Not sure	**47**	41	53	49	38	33	51
How much respect do you have for Jewish people generally?							
A lot of respect	**16**	18	15	16	14	14	17
A little respect	**4**	6	2	4	4	7	4
The same amount of respect as I have for anyone else	**59**	53	64	59	66	65	59
Not very much respect	**4**	4	4	4	2	2	4
No respect at all	**3**	4	2	3	4	0	4
Not sure	**14**	15	13	15	10	12	13

THINKING MORE ABOUT RESPECT FOR OTHERS...

	Total	Male	Female	18-34	35-54	Active in ISOC	Non-ISOC Member
How much respect do you have for atheists?							
A lot of respect	**6**	6	7	6	8	11	7
A little respect	**3**	4	2	3	2	4	3
The same amount of respect as I have for anyone else	**66**	63	70	66	68	65	66
Not very much respect	**6**	5	8	6	12	9	6
No respect at all	**5**	6	4	5	2	0	5
Not sure	**13**	16	11	14	8	12	13
And what about homosexuals?							
A lot of respect	**5**	5	6	6	4	9	6
A little respect	**4**	6	3	4	2	11	3
The same amount of respect as I have for anyone else	**53**	43	61	52	62	40	56
Not very much respect	**14**	16	13	15	12	19	14
No respect at all	**11**	16	6	11	6	9	10
Not sure	**13**	14	11	12	14	12	11

You may have heard a while ago about Gillian Gibbons, the British teacher in Sudan who was sent to prison for 15 days after naming a teddy-bear 'Mohammed'. Do you think her punishment was...?

	Total	Male	Female	18-34	35-54	Active in ISOC	Non-ISOC Member
Too harsh	**65**	60	70	65	64	56	67
Not harsh enough	**5**	8	3	5	4	9	5
About right	**11**	11	12	11	12	12	12
Not sure	**19**	21	16	19	20	23	16

97

Centre for Social Cohesion

	Total	Male	Female	18-34	35-54	Active in ISOC	Non-ISOC Member
All Muslim students	**632**	297	335	579	48	72	411
	%	%	%	%	%	%	%

Once you finish university, in which of the following regions would you most like to settle down and work? [If you intend to stay and work in the UK please indicate this in the list below.]

	Total	Male	Female	18-34	35-54	Active in ISOC	Non-ISOC Member
United Kingdom	**70**	67	72	71	60	70	69
Middle East	**4**	4	4	4	6	9	3
Asia (South Eastern)	**3**	3	2	3	0	4	3
Europe (Western) – excluding UK and the Republic of Ireland	**3**	3	2	2	8	2	3
America (Central)	**2**	2	2	2	0	2	2
America (North)	**2**	1	2	2	2	0	2
Europe (Eastern)	**2**	2	2	2	0	4	2
Africa (North)	**2**	2	2	2	0	2	1
Africa (Middle)	**1**	3	0	1	2	4	1
Africa (West)	**1**	2	1	1	4	0	1
Asia (Eastern)	**1**	0	2	1	0	0	2
Asia (Southern)	**1**	1	1	1	4	0	2
Europe (Northern)	**1**	2	0	1	2	0	2
Africa (East)	**1**	0	1	1	0	0	1
Asia (Western)	**1**	1	0	0	2	0	1
Australasia	**1**	0	1	0	4	0	1
Europe (Southern)	**1**	0	1	1	0	0	1
Other	**1**	1	1	1	0	2	1
Don't know	**5**	6	6	5	4	4	5

Non-Muslim students poll results

YouGov / Centre for Social Cohesion Survey Results*
Sample Size: 831
Fieldwork: 22nd - 29th January 2008

Centre for Social Cohesion	Total	Male	Female	18-34	35-54
All non-Muslim students	**831**	354	439	826	5
	%	%	%	%	%
Are you a member of any religious societies at your university?					
Yes	**6**	7	6	6	*40*
No	**93**	92	93	93	*60*
Not applicable – my university doesn't have any religious societies	**1**	1	2	2	*0*
And how active would you say you are in that society?					
I'm a committee member of the society	**20**	17	23	21	*0*
Very active – I go to all of the meetings and events	**14**	17	12	13	*50*
Fairly active – I go to most of the meetings and events	**22**	30	15	21	*50*
Not very active – I go to some meetings and events but not	**34**	26	39	35	*0*
Not at all active – I'm a member but I never attend meetings	**10**	9	12	10	*0*
Not sure	**0**	0	0	0	*0*
From what you know about your university's Islamic Society, which, if any, of the following statements do you generally agree with? [Please tick all that apply.]					
The Society is an important voice for religious students at my university	**58**	65	54	58	*50*
The Society tends to promote interfaith activities (e.g. between Muslims Jews Christians Hindus and Sikhs etc.)	**28**	39	19	27	*50*
There is some debate within the Society about the kind of ideas the society should promote	**24**	26	23	23	*50*
Some people within the Society have very different understandings of our religion	**30**	39	23	31	*0*
The Society tends to discourage interfaith activities (i.e. between Muslims Jews Christians Hindus and Sikhs etc.)	**4**	4	4	2	*50*
The Society is really just a chance for like-minded people to get together	**56**	48	62	58	*0*
None of these	**4**	4	4	4	*0*
Is it ever justifiable to kill in the name of religion?					
Yes in order to preserve and promote that religion	**1**	1	0	1	*0*
Yes but only if that religion is under attack	**1**	3	0	2	*0*
No it is never justifiable	**94**	92	97	94	*100*
Not sure	**4**	5	3	4	*0*

* Figures shown in italics denote findings which are too small to be statistically viable. On some occasions figures shown here will differ by 1% to those in part two where the raw results have been rounded up or down where appropriate.

Centre for Social Cohesion	Total	Male	Female	18-34	35-54
All non-Muslim students	**831**	354	439	826	5
	%	%	%	%	%

Thinking about your university friends, which of the following statements comes closest to describing your social group?

Culturally my university friends and I probably quite similar	**42**	39	45	42	0
I have friends at university from all sorts of different backgrounds	**55**	58	52	55	100
Not sure	**3**	3	3	3	0

To what extent, if at all, do you consider yourself to be 'British'?

I am British	**76**	73	78	76	100
I consider myself partially British and partially something else	**16**	17	15	16	0
I am not British	**5**	7	4	5	0
Not sure	**3**	3	4	3	0

Which, if any, of the following statements comes closer to your view?

Islam is a religion whilst Islamism is a political ideology	**41**	42	41	41	80
They are both part of the same thing – politics is a big part of Islam	**21**	27	16	21	20
Neither of these	**11**	13	11	11	0
Not sure	**26**	18	33	27	0

How supportive, if at all, would you be of the establishment of an Islamic political party to represent the views of Muslims at Parliament in Westminster?

Very supportive	**5**	6	4	5	20
Fairly supportive	**18**	16	21	18	20
Not very supportive	**26**	24	26	26	20
Not at all supportive	**35**	44	28	35	40
Not sure	**17**	11	21	17	0

And how supportive, if at all, would you be of the official introduction of Shari'ah Law into British law for Muslims in Britain?

Very supportive	**0**	1	0	0	20
Fairly supportive	**4**	4	3	4	0
Not very supportive	**15**	11	17	15	0
Not at all supportive	**61**	73	52	61	80
Not sure	**20**	11	27	20	0

To what extent, if at all, do you think Islam is compatible with the Western notion of democracy?

Very compatible	**4**	6	3	4	0
Fairly compatible	**30**	29	31	30	20
Fairly incompatible	**31**	33	27	31	20
Very incompatible	**20**	21	18	19	60
Not sure	**16**	11	21	16	0

Centre for Social Cohesion	Total	Male	Female	18-34	35-54
All non-Muslim students	**831**	354	439	826	5
	%	%	%	%	%

And how compatible, if at all, do you think Islam is with the separation of religion and government?

Very compatible	**3**	3	2	3	20
Fairly compatible	**17**	18	17	17	20
Fairly incompatible	**30**	32	26	30	0
Very incompatible	**26**	30	23	26	60
Not sure	**25**	17	31	25	0

How important to Islam do you think it is that Muslim women wear the hijab?

Very important	**18**	17	19	18	0
Fairly important	**36**	33	39	36	20
Not very important	**21**	24	18	20	60
Not at all important	**11**	15	8	11	20
Not sure	**14**	11	16	14	0

And in your understanding, how acceptable is it for men and women to associate freely in Muslim society?

Very acceptable	**8**	9	7	8	40
Fairly acceptable	**21**	22	21	21	20
Not very acceptable	**46**	43	48	46	40
Not at all acceptable	**14**	16	13	15	0
Not sure	**10**	10	11	10	0

From your understanding of Islam, are men and women considered equal in the eyes of Allah?

Yes they are	**11**	11	12	11	40
Yes except one or two issues	**15**	15	15	15	0
No not really	**36**	35	35	36	20
No not at all	**25**	27	24	25	40
Not sure	**13**	12	14	13	0

And in your experience of British society, are Muslim men and women treated equally?

Yes they are	**9**	10	8	9	20
Yes except on one or two issues	**23**	26	20	23	0
No not really	**40**	38	42	40	60
No not at all	**16**	16	16	16	20
Not sure	**12**	9	14	12	0

To what extent to do you agree or disagree that Muslims serving in the British armed forces should have the right to opt out of the army if they are required to fight in Muslim countries?

Strongly agree	**3**	3	3	3	40
Tend to agree	**15**	11	17	15	20
Tend to disagree	**29**	27	31	30	0
Strongly disagree	**42**	53	34	42	40
Not sure	**11**	6	15	11	0

101

Centre for Social Cohesion	Total	Male	Female	18-34	35-54
All non-Muslim students	**831**	354	439	826	5
	%	%	%	%	%

And to what extent do you agree or disagree that NON-Muslims serving in the British armed forces should have the right to opt out of the army if they are required to fight in certain areas?

Strongly agree	**3**	3	3	3	20
Tend to agree	**15**	11	18	15	40
Tend to disagree	**31**	26	35	31	20
Strongly disagree	**40**	52	31	40	20
Not sure	**11**	7	14	11	0

How has Britain's involvement with the war in Iraq affected the amount of respect you have for the British government?

My respect has increased	**2**	3	2	2	0
My respect has decreased	**53**	50	55	53	80
No change: I respected the British government anyway	**17**	22	13	17	20
No change: I didn't respect the British government anyway	**16**	17	16	17	0
Not sure	**11**	8	13	11	0

And how has the British public's reaction to the war in Iraq affected the amount of respect you have for British SOCIETY?

My respect has increased	**14**	15	12	14	0
My respect has decreased	**28**	32	24	28	60
No change: I respected British society anyway	**27**	28	27	28	20
No change: I didn't respect British society anyway	**10**	11	9	10	20
Not sure	**22**	15	28	22	0

How much respect do you have for atheists generally?

I am an atheist	**28**	30	28	28	0
A lot of respect	**8**	9	6	7	20
A little respect	**2**	3	1	2	0
The same amount of respect as I have for anyone else	**56**	52	59	56	60
Not very much respect	**2**	3	1	2	0
No respect at all	**0**	0	1	0	20
Not sure	**4**	3	4	4	0

How much respect do you have for Muslims generally?

I am a Muslim	**0**	0	0	0	0
A lot of respect	**8**	7	9	8	20
A little respect	**5**	7	4	5	20
The same amount of respect as I have for anyone else	**75**	73	77	75	40
Not very much respect	**7**	9	6	7	20
No respect at all	**2**	3	1	2	0
Not sure	**3**	2	3	3	0

Centre for Social Cohesion	Total	Male	Female	18-34	35-54
All non-Muslim students	**831**	354	439	826	5
	%	%	%	%	%

How much respect do you have for Jewish people generally?

I am Jewish	**1**	1	0	1	0
A lot of respect	**9**	10	9	9	20
A little respect	**4**	5	3	4	0
The same amount of respect as I have for anyone else	**81**	76	84	81	40
Not very much respect	**3**	4	1	2	40
No respect at all	**1**	1	1	1	0
Not sure	**2**	2	2	2	0

How much respect do you have for gay / lesbian people generally?

I am gay / lesbian	**5**	9	2	5	0
A lot of respect	**11**	9	13	11	20
A little respect	**2**	4	1	2	0
The same amount of respect as I have for anyone else	**77**	72	80	77	60
Not very much respect	**3**	3	2	3	20
No respect at all	**1**	1	1	1	0
Not sure	**1**	2	1	1	0

103

Centre for Social Cohesion	Total	Male	Female	18-34	35-54
All non-Muslim students	**831**	354	439	826	5
	%	%	%	%	%

Once you finish university, in which of the following regions would you most like to settle down and work?
[If you intend to stay and work in the UK please indicate this in the list below.]

	Total	Male	Female	18-34	35-54
United Kingdom	**69**	64	73	69	40
Africa (East)	**0**	0	0	0	0
Africa (Middle)	**0**	0	1	0	0
Africa (North)	**0**	0	0	0	0
Africa (South)	**0**	0	0	0	0
Africa (West)	**0**	0	0	0	0
America (Central)	**0**	0	0	0	0
America (North)	**6**	7	4	6	0
America (South)	**0**	1	0	0	0
Asia (Central)	**0**	0	0	0	0
Asia (Eastern)	**1**	1	1	1	0
Asia (South Eastern)	**0**	0	1	0	0
Asia (Southern)	**0**	0	0	0	0
Asia (Western)	**0**	0	0	0	0
Australasia	**4**	5	3	4	0
Caribbean	**1**	1	0	1	0
Europe (Eastern)	**1**	1	1	1	0
Europe (Northern)	**2**	2	2	2	20
Europe (Southern)	**1**	1	1	1	0
Europe (Western) – excluding UK and the Republic of Ireland	**6**	6	6	6	20
Ireland (Republic of)	**1**	1	1	1	0
Melanesia	**0**	0	0	0	0
Micronesia	**0**	0	0	0	0
Middle East	**0**	0	0	0	20
Polynesia	**0**	0	0	0	0
Other	**1**	0	1	1	0
Don't know	**7**	9	6	7	0

Friends of Al-Aqsa Literature

Literature produced by Friends of Al-Aqsa and often distributed by the Federation of Student Islamic Societies is available at many UK campuses.[72] Below is a sample of material found on UK campuses during the academic year 2007/2008.

Title:

"Al-Aqsa Mosque Under Attack 1967 to 2006"

Description:

The leaflet argues that, according to an international ruling, Al-Aqsa belongs to the Palestinian people. It includes a lengthy timeline, detailing the alleged attacks on Al-Aqsa by the Israeli Defence Forces, Israeli government and individuals. The leaflet is predominantly aimed at people who have little knowledge of the conflict. The front cover has a picture of Al-Aqsa mosque.

Found:

ISOC Table, Freshers' Fair, University of Birmingham, 27th Sept 2007

Title:

"Boycott Apartheid Israel"

Description:

The leaflet briefly argues for an economic boycott of Israeli companies and those that support Israel, listing a suggestive list of companies that should be boycotted. Some non-Israeli companies are listed purely based on economic ties with Israel, whilst others are done so because a company's chairman or CEO is a supposed "Zionist". It equates Israel's treatment of Palestinians with South Africa's apartheid regime. The leaflet is aimed at a general audience.

Found:

Brothers' Prayer Room, Students' Guild, University of Birmingham, 27th September, 2007

Sisters' Prayer Room, Students' Guild, University of Birmingham, 11th January, 2008

Brothers' prayer room, School of Oriental and African Studies (SOAS) 11th September, 2007

---

72 More Friends of Al-Aqsa literature is available on their website, www.aqsa.org.uk, in the resources section.

Title:

"Boycott Israeli Academic Institutions"

Description:

The leaflet argues that Israeli academic institutions should be boycotted because the Israeli government has shut down the Palestinian education system. The leaflet iterates that a boycott would be largely symbolic. It lists a series of "violations" allegedly carried out by Israel, from physical attacks on students (listed as 501 between 2000 and 2004) to propaganda attacks on the Palestinian education system. It is aimed at a general audience.

Found:

Brothers' Prayer Room, Students' Guild, University of Birmingham, 27th September, 2007

Sisters' Prayer Room, Students' Guild, University of Birmingham, 11th January, 2008

Title:

"Children of Palestine"

Description:

A short leaflet detailing attacks on Palestinian children, giving examples of deaths that have occurred at the hands of Israeli 'snipers'. Because other children have to witness this, the leaflet argues, their education has been impeded due to psychological trauma. It details statistics on the demographics of Palestinian children, those suffering from malnutrition and poverty as well as those killed during the intifada. The front cover shows a picture of children standing in front of a tank. Facts are unsourced and the leaflet is aimed predominantly at those who have little knowledge of the Israeli-Palestinian conflict.

Found:

ISOC Table, Freshers' Fair, University of Birmingham, 27th Sept 2007

Title:

"Christians in the Holy Land Today"

Description:

The leaflet highlights that Palestinian Christians co-existing peacefully and happily with Palestinian Muslims, taking the position that Christians are just as affected by the state of Israel as are Muslims. The leaflet also contains an application form for new members and donations to Friends of Al-Aqsa. It seems to be aimed at Muslims and Christians.

Found:

Brothers' Prayer Room, Students' Guild, University of Birmingham, 27th September, 2007

Title:

"Dome of the Rock: Qubbat – As Sakhra"

Author:

Ismail Patel, Friends of Al-Aqsa

Description:

The booklet gives general information about the Al-Aqsa mosque, including its archaeological structure and historical origins. The last page of the booklet asks readers to help publicise the 'plight of the Palestinians and [safeguard] Masjid al Aqsa'. The back of the booklet details other publications about Palestine. The book is aimed at a general audience, both Muslims and non-Muslims.

Found:

Sisters' Prayer Room, Students' Guild, University of Birmingham, 11th January, 2008

ISOC Table, Freshers' Fair, University of Birmingham, 27th September, 2007

Title:

"Friends of Al-Aqsa"

Description:

The leaflet outlines the background of the Friends of Al-Aqsa group and then sets out its manifesto and its activities. It contains an application to become a member or donate money, detailing why one should join Al-Aqsa, such as supporting the human rights of Palestinians and to redress 'a racist apartheid regime'. It is aimed at a general audience.

Found:

Brothers' Prayer Room, Students' Guild, University of Birmingham, 27th September, 2007

Title:

"Illegal Israeli Settlements"

Description:

The leaflet criticises Israeli settlements, particularly those surrounding Jerusalem and Bethlehem, in the West Bank. It labels the settlements as illegal by citing some of the articles of the Geneva Convention that the settlements allegedly violate. The leaflet is also written from the perspective of Palestinians, illustrating the settlements' impact on their lives and livelihoods. It is aimed at a general audience.

Found:

Brothers' Prayer Room, Students' Guild, University of Birmingham, 27th September, 2007

Title:

"Isolating Bethlehem"

Description:

This pamphlet explores the effect of the Israeli security wall on the Palestinian people, particularly in reference to Bethlehem. The pamphlet seems geared towards Christian readers, as it focuses predominantly on how the wall is preventing Christians (Palestinians and tourists alike) from accessing Bethlehem. The pamphlet quotes Pope John Paul II saying "The Holy Land does not need walls, but bridges".

Found:

Brothers' prayer room, School of Oriental and African Studies (SOAS) 11th September, 2007

Title:

"Israel – Palestine: Facts"

Description:

This leaflet describes the devastation Israel has caused in the Palestinian Territories, giving a historical background and relating the process of appropriation of land and resources from Palestinian control. The leaflet states that some of Israel's actions are illegal under international law, and concludes that "Israel is now officially an apartheid state". The leaflet is aimed at a general audience.

Found:

Sisters' Prayer Room, Students' Guild, University of Birmingham, 11th January, 2008

Brothers' prayer room, School of Oriental and African Studies (SOAS) 11th September, 2007

Title:

"Israeli Apartheid Policies"

Description:

The pamphlet details alleged "Israeli apartheid policies". It does not refer to relations between Muslims and non-Muslims, but rather to relations between Palestinians and Israeli security forces. The pamphlet also draws parallels between Israeli and Palestinian relations to apartheid South Africa. The pamphlet lists various "Israeli apartheid policies", detailing their supposed effects on the Palestinian people. The pamphlet begins and ends with quotations from Archbishop Desmond Tutu. It is aimed at a general audience.

Found:

Brothers' Prayer Room, Students' Guild, University of Birmingham, 27th September, 2007

Brothers' prayer room, School of Oriental and African Studies (SOAS) 11th September, 2007

Title:

"Palestinian Prisoners Held by Israel"

Description:

The leaflet details the imprisonment of Palestinians in Israeli prisons that has risen from 650,000 in 1967 to 8,000 today. Citing case studies including those of children, the leaflet calls for international support for Palestinian prisoners, arguing that they are tortured and deprived of basic human rights. It is aimed at a general audience.

Found:

Brothers' Prayer Room, Students' Guild, University of Birmingham, 27th September, 2007

Sisters' Prayer Room, Students' Guild, University of Birmingham, 11th January, 2008

ISOC Table, Freshers' Fair, University of Birmingham, 27th September, 2007

Title:

"Israel Divest and Boycott"

Description:

The leaflet calls for the boycott of Israel and for the need to divest. It compares apartheid South Africa to the situation in Israel and lists a number of international laws and UN resolutions that Israel is allegedly violating, which forms the basis of pamphlet's argument. The leaflet also highlights the decision of some religious groups in the UK and US to divest, and argues for an academic boycott of Israel and other points of action. The leaflet is aimed at a general audience.

Found:

Brothers' prayer room, School of Oriental and African Studies (SOAS) 11th September, 2007

Title:

Poster – "The Wall: The Israeli Apartheid Wall"

Publishers:

Appears to be jointly published by Friends of Al-Aqsa and the Federation of Student Islamic Societies

Description:

This poster aims to inform the viewer, Muslims and non-Muslims, about the Israeli wall enclosing the West Bank, portraying it as out-of-line with international norms. It seems aimed at a general audience, perhaps Christians and non-Muslims in particular given its reference to apartheid and a quote from John Paul II.

The poster makes the following statements: "The wall will run 700 km deep inside the West Bank; Over 200,000 Palestinians living in 67 towns and villages will suffer the direct impact of the Wall; Over 50% of the West Bank will be annexed by the Wall; According to international law the Wall is a 'Crime Against Humanity'; The Israeli wall will be 700 km long while the Berlin Wall was 154 km long; The Israeli Wall is in-part 8m high the Berlin Wall was 3.6 m high; The Israeli Wall has been ruled illegal by the International Court of Justice." At the bottom of the poster a quote attributed to Pope John Pal II reads, "The Holy Land does not need walls, but bridges."

A drawn image shows a section of concrete wall specified as "in places 8m high", with fences, ditches and barbed wire on either side. A tank stands on the West Bank side, while on the Israeli side a military car drives past. A colour-coded map inset shows the barrier's planned route compares its impact on different areas of the West bank. There are accompanying photos of a tall section of wall.

Found:

Brothers' prayer room, School of Oriental and African Studies (SOAS) October, 2007 – material appeared to be leftover from the SOAS ISOC Freshers' Fair.

Title:

"The Wall"

Description:

The leaflet begins by stating facts on the construction of the security wall that have been sourced to www.stopthewall.org. The leaflet then explores the impact of the wall on Palestinians' lives both socially and economically before listing the international laws and articles that the wall violates. The leaflet is aimed largely at non-involved people. It does not specifically refer to Muslims and non-Muslims but rather the Palestinian people and Israel.

Found:

Brothers' prayer room, School of Oriental and African Studies (SOAS) 11th September, 2007

Students' Guild, University of Birmingham, 27th September 2007,

Brothers' Prayer Room, Muslim Students Centre (Green Room), Leeds University, 18th September, 2007,

ISOC Table, Freshers' Fair, University of Birmingham, 27th Sept 2007,

List of universities visited

The University of Birmingham

City University London

Imperial College London

King's College London (KCL)

The University of Leeds

The University of Leicester

London School of Economics (LSE)

The University of Manchester

Queen Mary

School of Oriental and African Studies (SOAS)

University College London (UCL)

University of Westminster

The authors

John Thorne is a researcher with the think-tank Civitas, which founded the Centre for Social Cohesion in 2007. Previously, he served as North Africa Reporter for The Associated Press, and was a freelance correspondent based in Beirut and London. His work has appeared in The Christian Science Monitor, the San Francisco Chronicle, Haaretz, and other publications. He is also a Contributing Editor of The Liberal. Thorne holds a BA in philosophy from Whitman College and an MA in Mediterranean Studies from King's College London.

Hannah Stuart is a researcher at the Centre for Social Cohesion. She holds a BA in English from the University of Bristol and an MA in International Studies and Diplomacy from the School of Oriental and African Studies.

Acknowledgements

The authors would like to thank all those interviewed, Stephen Shakespeare and Kate Davies from YouGov, Salam Hafez, Joshua Segal, Ben Levitt, George Readings, Maariya Arshad as well as James Brandon, Houriyah Bashir and Robin Simcox from the Centre for Social Cohesion.

The Centre for Social Cohesion

The Centre for Social Cohesion is an independent and non-partisan think-tank based in London. It was founded by Civitas in 2007 to promote new thinking that can help bring Britain's ethnic and religious communities closer together while strengthening British traditions of openness, tolerance and democracy. The CSC is the first think-tank in the UK to specialise in studying radicalisation and extremism within Britain.